TOWARDS
THE LOST PARADISE

TOWARDS
the
LOST PARADISE

M. Fethullah Gülen

KAYNAK

Published by

Kaynak (Izmir) A.S.

871 Sokak No. 47

Konak-Izmir/TURKEY

Printed and bound in Turkey
by Caglayan A.S.

Contents

ABOUT THE AUTHOR

Known by his simple and austere life-style, Fethullah Gülen is one of the leading scholars and thinkers of present Turkey. Born in 1938 in Erzurum, Eastern Turkey, he had his formal and religious education in his village and Erzurum. Upon graduation from Divinity school he obtained his licence to preach and teach in a relatively young age.

Fethullah Gülen began to teach in Edirne in 1958. As well as teaching, he also took part, throughout this period, in other social services. After doing his military service and teaching for some time more in Edirne, he was transferred to Izmir, the third biggest province in Turkey. His appointment to Izmir was to prove a turning-point. Since childhood he had been totally dedicated to religious life and deeply interested in the condition of not only Muslims but also of the whole of mankind. While in Izmir, he never restricted himself to teaching in a single place. He began to travel from city to city to give lectures on subjects ranging from Darwinism to social justice in Islam.

Fethullah Gülen had long dreamed of a young generation who would combine intellectual 'enlightenment' with pure spirituality, wisdom and continuous activisim. Being extraordinarily knowledgeable in religious and social sciences and quite familiar with the principles of 'material' sciences, he was able to instruct his students in almost all of them. The first students who attended his courses in Izmir became the vanguard of the revived generation willing to serve his ideals. The small group that had begun to form around the opinions of Fethullah Gülen by the end of 1960s has increased rapidly ever since. This generation has rendered, and still continues to render, services to people without expecting any material reward. These services include teaching, establishing private institutions of education all over the world, publishing books, magazines, dailies and weeklies, TV and radio broadcasts, and funding scholarships for poor students. The daily they publish appears in sixteen countries and is ready to appear in many more others and the broadcast of the TV channel they run covers a wide area stretching from Turkey to India and the Middle East.

Fethullah Gülen unequivocally believes and asserts that if you wish to serve people in the best way possible simply starve them for knowledge. Only way to get out from under tyranny and attain to human perfection is through the attainment of knowledge. Totally dedicated to solving the society's problems, he believes the road to justice for all is paved with an adequate universal education. Only then would there be sufficient understanding and tolerance in the society to show respect for the rights of others. To this end, he has over the years, encouraged society's elite and the community leaders, industrialists and business leaders in his community to support quality education for the needy.

His tireless efforts in this area have begun to bear fruit for the society, as the people captivated by his sincere calls have founded hundreds of institutions of education, including dormitories, primary, secondary and high schools, universities and the institutions to prepare high school graduates for university education. These institutions are already found in more than fifty countries from England to Australia and the United States and from Russian cities such as Petersburg and Moscow to Yakutsky, including all of the Middle Asian countries whether independent or in the Russian Federation, and therefrom to South Africa. The students from the private schools in Turkey and Central Asia have taken top honours in university placement tests and consistently finished at the top in International Knowledge Olympics, producing a number of world champions, especially in sciences, such as maths, physics, chemistry, and biology.

Fethullah Gülen is also well-known for his ardent endeavours to strengthen bonds among all peoples of the world. He maintains that the bonds among the people of not only an individual country but the whole world are much more than those separating them. So, there should be established a sincere, strong dialogue and tolerance among them. To this end, he pioneered in the establishment of a foundation called the Foundation of Journalists and Writers, the activities of which to promote dialogue and tolerance among all strata of the society receive warm welcome from almost all walks of life. Again to this end, Fethullah Gülen visits and receives especially leading figures not only from the Turkish people, but from all over the world. In Turkey, the Vatican Ambassador to Turkey, the Patriarch of the Turkish Orthodox people, the Patriarch of the Turkish Armenian community, the Chief Rabbi of the Turkish Jewish community and many others including leading journalists, columnists, TV and movie stars and thinkers of varying views, are among those with whom he frequenty meets. As a historical step to interreligious and intercivilizational dialogue, he visited the Pope in Vatican and received the leaders of the World Council of Churches and religious leaders of the Jews in the world, including the Chief Rabbi of Israel.

With his acute perception, Fethullah Gülen feels the positive change in the spiritual climate in the world. He envisons a 21st century in which we shall witness the sprouting of a spiritual dynamic that will dust off the moral values dormant for so long. He envisons the birth of the age of tolerance and understanding leading to the co-operation of civilizations and ultimately to the fusion of the two into one body. Human spirit shall triumph in the way to intercivilizational dialogue and sharing of values.

'Today's man is in search of his Creator and the purpose of his creation', Fethullah Gülen contends. To questions, *Why was I born? What is the purpose of my living? What is the meaning of death and what does it demand from me?* he gives very practical yet singularly convincing answers. In his speeches and writings one encounters statements like 'Man has come to a crossroads, one leads to despair, the other to salvation; may God give us the wisdom to make the right choice.' In his daily life, man must maintain a delicate balance between material and spiritual values, he emphasizes. Only then could man enjoy serenity and true happiness.

The intellectuals and scholars of present Turkey who know him acknowledge Fethullah Gülen as one of the most serious and important thinkers and writers, and among the wisest activists, of twentieth-century Turkey or even of the Muslim world. According to him, in today's enlightened world, the only way to get others accept your ideas is by persuasion through convincing arguments. Therefore, during his whole life-time which has passed in privation but by studying, teaching, travelling, writing, speaking, and always deeply and inwardly feeling for the sufferings of both intellectually and spiritually bankrupt and materially oppressed peoples of the world, he has brought up many scholarly people, and still continues his teaching in private. He has thousands of tape and video cassettes on which his sermons and discourses have been recorded, and many books mostly compiled from his articles, sermons, and the answers he has given to different questions asked him in different times. Some of his books are as follows:

Asrin Getirdigi Tereddutler (4 volumes; vol. 1 has appeared in English translation as *Questions This Modern Age Puts to Islam)*

Cag ve Nesil ('This Era and the Young Generation')

Zamanin Altin Dilimi ('The Golden Part of Time')

Renkler Kusaginda Hakikat Tomurcuklari (translated as *Truth through Colors)*

Kirik Mizrap ('Broken Plectrum'), a collection of verse.

Fatiha Uzerine Mulahazalar ('The Interpretation of *Sura al-Fatiha')*

Olcu Veya Yoldaki Isiklar (4 volumes; vo. 1 has appeared in English traslation as *Criteria or the Lights of the Way)*

The present book is composed of Fethullah Gülen's selected articles which have so far been published in different magazines. In these articles, you will travel through the vivid expressions of Mr. Gülen and see the collapse of a magnificent civilization and inward decay of Muslim peoples all over the world, and you will witness the sigh of a Muslim scholar over the miserable conditions of Muslims. The flowery language of Fethullah Gülen will at times take you through a different world, the happy world of the future, where flowers sway on sloping hills and birds sing of spring everywhere, and you will come to know how it can be possible to found such a world.

***

THE JOURNEY BEYOND BEING

O God, Most High,

We behold the spectacle that You have laid out before us, Your most original and striking works made in the most perfect form, to which You invite our gaze. We behold things and events that, in their inter-relation, are the most brilliant and well-proportioned of Your dazzling pictures. The manifestation of all Your beauties draws out from the bosom of nature a variety of colours unfolding as if in a book of art. Bearing witness to You by the writing of Your Pen, and in accordance with Your Book which You have written with that Pen, our spirits have taken wing and we have gained sight of the source of all things in the light of Your Names. Voices and music of celestial harmonies are heard everywhere, and our hearts are ravished by the mystery of the sacred archetypes, which are the fountain of all things.

Through the eye of the heart we have grasped the essential identity between the kernel of belief and the *touba* tree of Paradise. We have risen to make a journey extending far into the realms beyond being. On this journey Your holy Book has been the guide to our spirits, setting out a vision of Your Names and Attributes and leading to eternity. You have described to us the journey to Yourself, and mapped it out in the minutest detail and pictured it in the *mi'raj* of Your holy Servant, peace and Your blessings be upon him, his miraculous ascent through the

Seven Heavens to Your Presence. That journey is possible to any man of gnosis through his spirit, but if we have gone too far in touching the latch of the gates of Your mysteries, then we ask forgiveness for the discoutersies of our coarse, unripened souls, ignorant of rules or proprieties.

O Creator, Most High and Most Beautiful, who brought us into this existence and allowed us to feel the infinite pleasure thereof. You have opened to us vast worlds as a book. You have made our consciousness the shore at which Your Divine mysteries lap, and so enabled us to have some sense of those mysteries. If You had not unfolded to us as in a book these magnificent worlds, if You had not disclosed Yourself to us, according to our capacity to understand, by sending Prophets, we would not have known You at all. If You had not established connections between nature and our inner experiences and endowed us with an innate perception by means of which we might arrive at true knowledge and true gnosis, we could never hope to know Your Divine Essence or anything sure about You, and how could we otherwise have felt admiration for Your Path? We are Your bonded servants, and the recurrent flashes reflected in our consciousness are rays from Your Existence. Whatever we own is entirely by Your gift and favour. We declare this once more, confessing that we are Your obedient slaves, who never look for release, but rather long to renew our bonds.

O Ruler of hearts, on remembrance and meditation of whom hearts are fixed, we strive to determine the ways which lead to Your Presence and the windows opening upon Your Existence. Sometimes we seek by delving into the reality of things and events, and sometimes by relying upon our intuitions. Our aim is to communicate what we receive from You to those whose hearts are sick and whose minds are barren, and to remain faithful to the sublime truths, which have been shown there in the clearest way.

No doubt we have committed errors and indulged our fancies and whims, for we have not been able to offer the most manifest truths in their essential purity.

If we have made mistakes, we made them while seeking You and trying to guide others. If we have made mistakes, we have made them on the way to You. But a mistake is still a mistake. With broken hearts, spirits doubled up, and necks in chains, we appeal to Your generous judgement. We make this confession, knowing that Your unbounded Mercy has always overcome Your Wrath. It is not becoming to Your humble slaves that they should commit faults, especially those You have favoured. Yet, since they do, graciously permit me to remark that mercy and forgiveness are becoming most of all to You.

O Ruler of my heart – 'To the Ruler belongs the Royal manner which befits Him, just as servitude befits a slave' – if You forgive us, we should wish to study the book of Your universe anew so as to hearken to the voices that tell of You; we should wish to witness the signs of Your Existence, and to be enraptured by the songs about You, so that we may reach Your holy realm. By Your Graciousness, assist in their efforts those in need!

TOWARDS THE WORLD
OF 'RIGHTEOUS SERVANTS'

God promises the final inheritance of the world to His righteous servants. So, in order to have a right to this promised inheritance, there must be a group of righteous people. What are the criteria of righteousness, or what qualities should the heir possess, to whom the final dominion of the earth was promised by God?

The first and foremost quality of the heir is perfect *faith*. The Qur'an determines the purpose of man's creation to be belief in God, which is woven from the threads of the knowledge of God, love, enthusiasm and spiritual fulfilment.

Indeed, it is only in the light of faith that man, by realizing his essential nature with all its dimensions and the existential aims of creation, can penetrate the inner reality of existence. Contrary to this, lack of belief is a suffocating dungeon. In the view of an unbeliever, existence began with chaos, developed in the frightening uncertainties of coincidences, and is speeding towards a terrible end. In this uncertain movement of existence, there is neither a breath of compassion to relieve us, nor a place of security to embrace us in our human desires, nor even a piece of ground to step on.

A believer who knows from where he came from and the destination of his life, together with his responsibilities, sees everything as clearly as 'daylight' and, because of this, he travels to his destination in utmost security. During his sojourn, he carefully studies existence and what lies behind existence. He examines things and events over and over again and tries to establish a connection with everything around him. He never refrains from making use of the studies of others and, where he lacks in sufficient knowledge and experience, goes on with his researches, without tiring and losing hope.

There is an inexhaustible source of power on which a believer relies during his travel – *there is no strength and power save with God*. This phrase is a source of power which a man who has obtained it, feels no need for another. A believer who has equipped himself with this source of power aims for none but God. He leads his life to secure His approval. He has an abiding optimism with which to overcome every obstacle and challenge all kinds of worldly opposition.

The second quality of the heir is to become overflowing with *love*. A person with a heart content with belief in and knowledge of God feels, in proportion to the degree of his belief and knowledge, a deep love for all human beings and even the whole creation. It is this person who spends his whole life-span in the colourful fluctuations of universal ecstasies, raptures and spiritual pleasure.

Today, as in every era, there is need for hearts to be enraptured with love and overflow with zeal so that a new revival could be realized. Without love, it is impossible to accomplish any permanent movement, especially if the movement is related to the Hereafter. The Divine love which we feel in order to gain God's approval is a boundless and mysterious source of power. The 'heirs to the earth' should never be heedless of this source and should make as much use of it as possible.

We need to look into the origin of existence from the perspective of the Qur'an and the example (*Sunnah*) of the noble Prophet, upon him be peace and blessings. The origin of man, his place in the universe, the Divine purpose for his creation, and the way he should conduct in his life as well as his final destination, are in such a harmony in these two sources – the Book and the *Sunnah* – with human thoughts and feelings and man's aspirations that we cannot help but be filled with wonder and admiration. These two pure sources are, for men of understanding, a spring of love and enthusiasm, and a means to ecstasy. Those who have recourse to them with pure intention and with petitions of needs are not refused, and those who take refuge in them gain immortality. They need to do so, however, with the sincerity of people like Imam Ghazali, Imam Rabbani, Shah Waliyullah and Bediuzzaman. They need to approach these sources with the excitement of Ghalib Dede and Mehmed Akif, and turn to them with the conviction and activity of Khalid, Salah al-Din, and Mehmet the Conqueror. Indeed, by combining the love and enthusiasm of those personages with modern methods and styles, we will penetrate into the ever-fresh essence of the Qur'an and arrive at a universal metaphysics.

To turn to sciences with a sensible synthesis of intellect, logic and consciousness is the third quality of the generation who were promised the final inheritance of the earth. This turning, which will also provide a direction for the general inclination of humanity, which is lost among some obscure hypotheses, will be a significant step in the liberation of mankind.

As pointed out by Bediuzzaman, mankind is increasingly concentrating on sciences and technology, driving all their strength from sciences. Bediuzzaman also pointed out that in order to present to the masses the product of scientific knowledge, eloquence and rhetoric will gain momentum and ascendancy. In fact, we no longer have any other way to escape from the cloudy atmosphere of illusions enveloping us. We no longer have any other way to reach truthls and, most importantly, the most manifest Truth.

In order to compensate for the last few centuries, it is necessary to rise to the highest level of scientific knowledge and, by removing the inferiority complex from our subconsciousnes, to realize self-assertion. To achieve this, we must re-evaluate sciences in the light of the prism of the Islamic thought and become unique representatives of scientific knowledge.

Since we have not been able so far to assign a true direction for sciences and, consequently, confused revealed knowledge with scientific theories, and sometimes scientific knowledge with philosophy, serious confusions have appeared in scientific thought and scientists have lost considerable esteem. In Turkey, this void were exploited by foreigners very well and many foreign schools sprouted up. The younger generations, as a result, were alienated from their society. After a while, these inexperienced generations lost all their religious and moral values, with the result that as a whole nation we were all degraded in thought, ideals, art and life. In the schools foreigners or native minorities established and ran, to which we entrusted our children without any worries, Western culture and values were given priority over science and scientific thought. It is for this reason that our young generations, although they had to cope with the age in science and technology, split into different parties like Marxism, Durkheimism, Leninism, and Maoism. Some consoled themselves with the dreams of a communist system and the dictatorship of the proletariat. Some were carried away by the existentialism of Sartre, Marcuse, Camus, and the like. Indeed, we witnessed in this land all such deviations, all of which were unfortunately nursed and promoted in supposed centres of science and knowledge. Meanwhile, religion and religious people were unceasingly attacked by destructive representatives of unenlightenment, and evil aspects of modern Western civilization were propagated. It is impossible for us to forget that dark period of our history and those who were responsible for it will always be remembered as the national and historical criminals in the conscience of people.

What remains now is to build a happy, bright future. This requires us to realize a revival through scientific thought which we have to inculcate in the minds of the young generation. The suffering of the people on account of what befell them in the past, the exasperation produced in their hearts by servility to foreign powers, and the national reaction to centuries of exploitation, cause us to sigh and lament in equal proportion to the regret of Adam, the weeping of Yunus (Jonah) and the pains of Ayyub (Job), upon them be peace. Such thoughts and feelings together with historical experiences stimulate and guide us to further exertions towards our destination.

The fourth characteristic of the generation to whom the final inheritance of the earth belongs is *to review and re-evaluate the established views of man, life and the universe.* The following points should be considered in this respect:

Firstly, the universe is a book written by God for us to study over and over again. Man is a transparent index of all the worlds, a being able to discover the depths of existence. As for life, it is the manifestation of the meanings filtered from that index and book, and reflected by Divine Expression throughout the universe. If man, life and the universe are three aspects of a single reality with each having a genuine colour of its own, then a partial approach to them will be a disrespect to both man, in particular, and the whole creation, in general, as it will demolish the harmonious composition of reality.

As it is indeed incumbent upon man to study, understand and obey the Divine Revelation – the Scripture – derived from God's Attribute of Speech, so too it is necessary for him to perceive all things and events to which God gives existence through His Knowledge, Will and Power. Being the manifestation of the Divine Attribute of Speech, the glorious Qur'an is the spirit of existence and the sole means of happiness in this world and the Hereafter. The 'Book' of the universe is the embodiment of this spirit and is an account of the branches of science originating in it. It is therefore a very important dynamic of both worlds, direct in relation to this life, indirect with respect to the other. For this reason, there will be a reward for understanding both of these books and applying their principles in practical life. Those who neglect or ignore them will meet the consequences of their neglect.

Secondly, a man's humanity lies in his feelings, thoughts and character, which are also the standards in determining his esteem in the sight of both the Creator and the created. Sublime human attributes, depth of thought and feeling, and a sound character, are valued by everybody. The one who adulterates his faith and conviction with irreligious thoughts and causes distrust in his character, will neither be able to receive God's support and help nor preserve his esteem and dignity in the sight of people. It should never be forgotten that God Almighty, as well as people, evaluates a man according to his human character, and who lack human values are not able to perform great feats even if they appear to be good believers. On the other hand, it is impossible for those who are distinguished with laudable virtues and a sound character to be always subject to utter failure despite their apparent weakness in living in conformity with religious principles.

Thirdly, an Islamic goal can be achieved through Islamic means and methods only. It is absolutely incumbent on a Muslim to pursue Islamic goals and adopt Islamic methods in attaining his goals. As it is impossible to secure God's approval without sincerity and purity of intention, so too, neither can Islam be served nor Muslims directed toward their real targets through diabolic means and methods.

The generation who will take on the responsibility of bringing justice and happiness to the world should be able *to think freely and respect freedom of thought.* Freedom is a significant dimension of man's free will and a key to the mysteries of human identity.

The Muslim world has been under pressure for centuries from both within and outside. Under such conditions where restrictions have been put on our feelings, thoughts, culture, and education, it is almost impossible for a person to remain with human faculties, let alone realize a renewal and development. In a climate where it is difficult to remain even as a common man with human values, it must be quite impossible to bring up a person of true greatness. Only people with weak character, inactive disposition, palsied brains and paralyzed feelings grow in such climates. Distorted thoughts and wrong criteria produced and propagated in both families and surroundings and in educational institutions and art circles in the later phase of our history, have upset everything unique to us – our view of matter and spirit and our physical and spiritual worlds. In this critical period, the leading élite presented their prejudices as free thought, lived an egocentric life, showed no respect for other beliefs and opinions, and went so far in maintaining different assertions or convictions that they did not refrain from resorting to force whenever they deemed it necessary to crush the free will and free thinking of the people. We are not sure whether that period has ended, though it remains necessary for us to review, on the one hand, our centuries-old historical dynamics and to question, on the other, the 'changes and transformations' to which we have given impetus for the last one and a half centuries. We are still, in our decisions, under some ideological taboos, in which case it is impossible for us to re-shape our world according to the requirements of a bright future. Such conditions as these give rise to nothing but political disputes, internal struggles and international conflicts. That is why there is a continuous internal discord in our community, in particular, and unceasing savagery worldwide, in general. Were it not for the egoism, greed and ruthlessness of mankind, the world would most probably be more different than it is today.

If this is so, we should realize the need to be more tolerant and more altruistic when we move forward toward a better future. We need today more than anything else magnanimous hearts and open, profound minds which are respectful of free thinking and open to the sciences and scientific research and which are able to perceive the harmony between the Qur'an and the Divine laws of the universe and life. This requires the existence of a community in which genius can flourish. In the past, a single person of genius could succeed in leading a nation toward high objectives, but today when everything has taken on an incredibly elaborate form, and specialization has gained prominence, *counsel and collective consciousness* have replaced geniuses. This is the sixth point which should be given due consideration by the generation who aim to give a better shape to the world.

We have not been able, in the latest phase of our history, to establish a desirable coordination between the vital institutions of the society. At a time when modern schools concentrated on ideological dogmas; institutions of religious education *(madrasas)* broke with life; institutions of spiritual training *(takyas)* were immersed in sheer metaphysics, and the army restricted itself to sheer force, this coordination was essentially not possible.

It is, indeed, a fact that modern schools could not save themselves from the influence of modern 'scholasticism' and ideological dogmas; institutions of religious education were closed to sciences and scientific thought, devoid of the spirit and the power to bring about new formations. The representatives of spiritual training lost their love and enthusiasm, consoling themselves with virtues and wonders of the saints who had lived in previous centuries. As for the army, which had once been the representative of the religious energy and activity and the symbol of national subsistence, it has developed the complex of self-assertion in the internal arena. Consequently, everything was upset, and the 'tree of nation' was convulsed so violently that it nearly toppled. Sadly it seems that, until the fortunate representatives of the bright future re-form these vital institutions in a way that they can perform their real functions, and bring forward the wedding of the mind and heart so as to make the ground propitious for the upbringing of the perfect man of thought, action and inspiration, such convulsions of different degrees will not cease.

Finally, the generation who aim to give a better shape to the world should be equipped with *mathematical thought*. Mathematical thought implies a comprehension of the enigmatic connection between creation and the 'laws' of mathematics, and a discovery of the mysterious world of numbers. Without mathematics, it is not possible to perceive the mutual relations between man and things; it is mathematics which, like a source of light, illuminates our way along the line from the universe to life and shows us the depths of the world of possibilities beyond human imagination, thus enabling us to attain our ideals.

In order to obtain a full perception of existence, we should follow the laws of mathematics in all fields from physics to mathematics, from matter to energy, from body to soul, and from law to spiritual training. This implies the need to adopt both spiritual training and scientific research. The West, in order to compensate for a real or true system of spiritual training, has had to have recourse to so-called mystical movements. But Muslims have no need to search for a foreign system to quench their thirst for spiritual satisfaction. Everything a person may need to design his life on sound foundations, scientific, spiritual, rational, sociological, economic, political and so on, can be found in Islam, provided that he is able to understand Islam in its pristine purity and original comprehensiveness.

Lastly, in oder to understand the *thought of art* which righteous servants whom God promised the final inheritance of the world, should have, we should have a much more developed intellectual capacity and refined feelings and sensitivity.

IN THE SHADE OF THE 'LIGHT' COMING FROM HEAVEN

I wonder whether we can study, as consciously and appreciatively as we should, this book of nature which stretches before us with its 'lines' 'embroidered in silk threads', and each page of which is an exhibition of different types of beauties. This brilliant and magnificent book, offered to us contemplation in the embrace of the sun, every season of it having a different beauty and elegance, is a source of reference and a mine of happiness and energy requiring careful analysis.

If we can study this book in the 'light' coming from heaven, and also in the light of the 'lamp' lit in our souls, and thereby feel elevated into the realms of existence on the wings of belief and knowledge, we will never fall into pessimism and feel loneliness. Rather, we will overflow with happiness each moment through a different 'pleasure'.

Stagnant waters become mossy; inactive limbs are subject to over-calcification. By contrast, waterfalls are always clean. Those who always keep their brains active and souls purified will one day see that they have germinated numerous 'seeds of beauty' in themselves and all their efforts have come to fruition. Only ploughed land can be sown; only gardens trimmed and trees pruned yield the best fruit.

As the nettles invading our gardens do so because of our neglect, so the malice we nourish is the outcome of our heedlessness. The active and vigilant souls look upon things and events through the windows of their pure thoughts and good feelings, and are united with the whole of existence. Why should they not be united with it, seeing that each thing or being is a 'word' brought into existence by the 'Pen of Divine Power'?

If we can look upon this world, where each living creature blossoms out and blooms, with the eyes of our hearts or souls, we will be able to see that every part of it is filled with the miraculous works of Divine Power: each tree, for example, is a lovely living organism in whose veins the life of water runs, and a worshipper of God which entreats Him with its arms – branches – opened; earth is ever-active with the excitement of new revivals at each moment, and through its co-operation with the sun, air and water, everywhere is covered with 'green' and moves to flowering and then fruiting.

If only man can remove the veil between his soul and eyes to see the reality of things, then the book of nature, which surrounds us with all its beauties, colours, smells, and dazzling designs, will be reflected in his soul and, saving him from the imprisonment of fancies and indulgences, take him through the corridors of Paradise. He will then find that everywhere he can reach with his sight and imagination is decorated with the most delicious of fruits and the most striking of views, in which his heart, spirit, eyes and ears will all have share to enrapture himself with happiness.

The Power that endowed us with the faculties of tasting and benefiting, has made our natural environment like gardens of Paradise. How splendid, then, it is to perceive the connection between Paradise and our natural environment to fill with spiritual effulgence, and how blessed and beneficial is the Hidden One Who enlightens us with every natural phenomenon.

The infinite beauty around us has displayed itself since the very beginning of the world, through each day, with ever-fresh blessings and meanings to point to Him. Through this ever-renewed display, these ever-fresh blossoms and meanings, like every other thing or being, man is also renewed and takes on different individualities. Those who live unaware of this renewal are blind and deaf to what happens around them. As for those who are fortunate enough to find themselves amidst the beauties of nature, they will dive into this abundant 'stream' and finally reach the 'ocean'.

Those blessed ones, each being a drop individually, but having become, through collective consciousness, like the 'ocean of existence' itself, will never feel loneliness and, unburdening themselves to their Creator, they will petition Him to 'heal' their 'wounds' and meet their needs. Their deep connection with Him will fly them to the innermost spheres of both their own and external existence, and they will attain the dazzling climes which eyes are unable to see, and minds to perceive.

The inner world of one who has discovered his being is as deep and bright as heavens, as vast as space and as colourful and heart-warming as gardens of Paradise. Through the torches he has lighted in his inner being, he sees all the veils removed from things and events and sees them enlightened.

Every truth appears, like a spark, in man with its own splendour and then, being ignited, becomes a flood of light, by which masses discover the ways to eternity, grasp the mystery of distances and are saved from bewilderment.

What now falls upon the fortunate generation who have realized both intellectual and spiritual enlightenment, is to convey to all parts of the world that Divine Light, which will provide people with a new perspective to evaluate things and events.

THE SAVIOUR AWAITED BY OUR GENERATION

Our young people are living in and through a most distressing period. The neglect of past centuries has brought to fruit the successive calamities we are experiencing now. The young have been buried under a heavy burden of anxiety with nothing of use coming to them from their fathers and mothers, from the home or the school, nothing whatever of any spiritual value.

The young, having been deprived of all traditional values, were crushed by the pressures of materialism. They showed no signs of purity or profundity of mind nor depth of feeling, nor spirituality. Such a thing was not at all unexpected given that the experience and traditions cultivated over a thousand years had been sacrificed to an adulterated, cosmopolitan culture.

The most painful and heart-rending aspect of the situation is that the intelligentsia, those who were expected to guide the community, readily adapted to the new low standard. It is difficult for us to comprehend how they could prefer an adulterated culture to the traditional one subtly formed over the centuries.

In just such conditions our young confronted the problems of coming to age! They were under great pressures resulting from the neglect of centuries. Their bewildered community had left the traditional ways, and a new force had appeared, but one that, not having suffered pangs of birth, was immature. The poor youth could not decide whom to follow and how could they decide, since they had never been given good examples, and had only seen those who fled from themselves in one way or another.

In a society going astray, which has suffered serious reverses, some had gone so far as to consider all ideas and traditions that had elevated their ancestors into a great nation as exhausted values. If only the young who were deprived of all the finer feelings had been able to understand what was happening around them!

That being the situation, what should we do to uplift a generation who have been turned from their origins, how should we inject new life into them? We have no right merely to complain about them or to criticize them for not reading or thinking. They were until very recently given no help at all, although they would have welcomed such help. We may not deny that some of them show a real desire to make serious researches or to learn. Others express that hunger by reading piles of newspapers or listening to the radio or watching television for hours to kill time or satisfy trivial desires. Also, although some of them gather around preachers to receive what there is to be received, we have, alas, been unable so far to give them anything worthwhile.

When have we guided the young to do the good and to choose the right? When have we been able to teach them to be virtuous? Do we have the ability to speak to them about a message given to make them think, study and reason? Can we be sure of the altruism of those who claim to lead and guide them to higher levels? How many men are there of stature and high standing who have renounced material and spiritual pleasures that we can point and look up to? They were waiting for a 'Hercules' who could say 'I have known nothing of worldly pleasures in my life of over eighty years', who would not change his life style until death. We need to find soldiers of God who will take on the sufferings of their generation without even thinking of the pleasures of Paradise. Alas, we have yet to find guides who would give up even worldly pleasures for the sake of the young.

It is true that we have not been able to help the young. We have not been able to find proper schools for them, nor to teach them the right way to integrate with the universe. They have been ground down by the teeth of events and, inevitably, have stood up in rebellion against those who put them in their state of wretchedness.

As in the picture showing a beheaded Goliath, they stand before those who took away their heads, demanding only the return of their souls. For them, to regain what they have lost is the most important thing.

Who will assume the heavy responsibility of returning to them what they have lost? The home? The society or its educational institutions? Under present circumstances none of these are up to the task, albeit certain individuals deserve to be encouraged. If we fail to provide facilities for the young to enable them to build their own world in accordance with the conditions of the real world, our failure will lead on to their destruction. The present state, notably of our educational institutions, is by no means promising. Neither our system of education, which has been degenerating little by little for centuries, nor our homes which are no more than kitchens and bedrooms, nor the society in general, which has been in a chaos, hold out much promise for the young.

The only way out is to develop a new understanding of science and to stimulate determination based on morality and insight, together with the cultivation of godliness. The new generation must be guided by a unity of mind, and take the true path in life, and they must regain their original, true identity. Besides, we must realize that we can only enable the young to reach such heights, and so save them from idleness and indifference, by inspiring them with idealism, by urging them to renounce merry-making in favour of the trials of 'becoming', by turning them away from self-indulgence and towards a love of others and of the homeland.

We pay homage to the fortunate ones who will shoulder so heavy a responsibility.

THE LEADING, EXALTED SPIRITS

Pure in mind, noble in character, healthy and active, deep-sighted and wise, full of humanitarian feelings towards the whole of mankind and love and compassion for their own people, the leading, exalted spirits are a small group of holy people who were leaders in history, and through whose messages time is freed from relativity and again through whose enlightenment the 'black holes' of space are changed into halls of Paradise.

Since they are bound together around a unique world-view and belief in one Object of Worship, and therefore are aware of the goal of their life, they are always at 'heights' and win victory after victory and honour after honour.

When they are occupied with their 'inner world', with nothing to excite them, they are extraordinarily calm and peaceful and so gentle that those who see them regard them as angels. But they are as hard and inflexible as steel when they are roused into fighting for their ideals. Without tiring, they gallop great distances to overcome all obstacles that appear before them. They continue firmly on their way, conveying their message until their guide tells them to stop.

They hold fast to their principles, compassionate towards each other and faithful to their leader, in whose hands each is like a sword of stainless steel. Dedicated to their cause, they strive for a whole lifetime seeking the pleasure of God in the service of their nation and humanity.

Even if their plans are upset, their forces destroyed, and discouraging misfortunes befall them one after the other, they are never shaken and, with a new, more vigorous attempt, they start on their way again in full submission to and total reliance upon God.

When they stand before God, each is so devoted a worshipper that those who see them, think they have completely renounced the world. But they thoroughly change when on battlefields and, although they never think of attacking first, once engaged, they give no respite to their enemies. Whatever aim they pursue, they never cease before obtaining it.

They hate the feeling of hatred and repel evil with what is the best. They never lower themselves to treat even their enemies meanly; instead, they find great pleasure in welcoming those they have conquered warmly and with a gentle manner.

They are reasonable and wise in all their acts and decisions. Their insight and discernment allow them to solve even the most intricate problems and they, therefore, implant hope and resolution in the hearts of even the most hopeless people. In strict avoidance of doing someone harm, they use all their strength, energy and abilities for the good of mankind.

They are deeply attached to their country and people, and they are ever ready to sacrifice themselves for their sake. Any misfortune befalling their people hurts them so deeply that they forget all worldly tastes and pleasures. In order to heal the wounds of the nation, they unceasingly inspire the young generations to awaken to lofty ideals, and they try to inculcate in them the spirit of struggle, and to equip them with the belief and resolution that an honourable death is preferable to a humiliating life.

The zeal to serve their nation in the way of their belief is so deeply implanted in their souls that they are preoccupied with it whether at school or in their military barracks, in fields or in shops, in an office or on the prayer mat, in the Parliament building or in a state or government office. They are very strong-willed and know how to get along with everyone. They always give priority to national matters over their own personal or family problems.

Their belief and conviction and their resolution and excitement are so formidable in resisting all the opposing powers and every kind of treasons that by them, they are able to surmount every obstacle and overcome every difficulty, however insurmountable they may seem.

Never falling into despair, they always abound with hope and energy trying to stop the cruelties of the world and to illuminate the whole universe. While others who live beyond their ambience of peace and happiness are drowned in a marsh of hopelessness, they strive in the way of founding a new world with abundance of hope and in directing people to new ways of revival.

THE HAPPY FUTURE

Life is possible only through hope;
The hopeless are distressed and unhappy.

M. Akif.

My eyes closed, I imagine the happy future being formed in the 'land of my hope'. Beauties of every sort coming out from corners of existence run through our houses and streets, and through institutions of education and worship, and military training, and then they are reflected back in the rooms of our houses, enveloping us in the form of a flood of light. Combined with colours, this light forms a rainbow, under which I run continuously to 'set it up' in my eyes and soul as an everlasting arch of happiness.

While we pass in a second under any arch set up on worldly occasions, it seems impossible to pass under this heavenly arch (rising) over us. As we run under it, we feel our life united with the whole of existence in an endless stream, and watch in amusement the things flowing back after a short halt on our either side to greet us, and replaced by new ones. We are enraptured with the immaterial pleasures coming from that continuous stream of things and intimacy between them and us.

Trees sway gently with breeze; hills are green and radiant; sheep pasturing here and there skip and bleat, and villages, big and small, scattered on slopes and in plains and valleys. We observe in delight how all these contribute to a universal harmony, and comment that a life-span is not enough to imbibe all these pleasures.

These colours and lights and sounds, and this liveliness springing from the breast of existence, are reflected in the world of our emotions, and we feel as if we were listening to lyrics composed of sweet day-dreams and memories flowing in waves. We absorb the vast book of nature arousing in us spiritual pleasures with its heaven containing the sun, the moon and stars, and its earth comprising mountains, plains, gardens, forests and rivers. This book fills us with indescribable delight and joy and elevates us to the higher realms of existence.

Each season we become as if we wakened from a different sleep of death and find ourselves before various colours ranging from purple to green. We feel caressed by breezes conveying the perfume of flowers and fruits and ears of grain.

These tremendous spectacles, which implant in souls the sense of beauty, give some relief even to those pessimists who always see everything through the window of their dark souls and are overwhelmed with evil thoughts and suspicions. As for the believing souls, time 'streams' in them echoing the melody of life in each cell of them. Mornings come upon them with the songs of gentle breezes through the leaves of trees, the murmur of streams, the twittering of birds and the cries of children. The sun sets in their horizon arousing in them different feelings of love and excitement, and nights take them, in various pitches of music, through the mysterious tunnels of time and most romantic spectacles of nature.

Every spectacle we observe within the horizon of belief and hope, and every voice we hear, removes all the veils from our souls and takes us through paradise valleys, radiant, soft, pure, serene and pleasant, in which time acquires infinity. This peace attracts us into fascinating worlds, half-seen, half-unseen, which we have long been watching with the eyes of our hearts as if from behind a 'lace curtain'.

At this point, when the spirit is enraptured with the pleasure of observation, the tongue keeps silence, eyes are closed and ears no longer receive sounds; everything is voiced with the tongue of the heart. Pure thoughts and feelings envelop man as vapour of joy and excitement, and, in the face of such dazzling spectacles, the spirit feels as if walking in gardens of paradise.

THE SPIRIT OF YOUTH

A community maintains its liveliness through the spirit of its young, and flourishes through it. When a community loses this spirit, it fades and withers away, like a flower whose veins have been cut, and it is finally crushed under foot.

A young man, of school age or in adolescence, is usually filled with activism, with national or patriotic feelings, talks about healing the wounds of the nation and developing the country, and is furious with idleness and insensitivity to the problems of the community. Nevertheless, many of the young who overflow with such lofty thoughts, usually settle down and lose this activism after they get a post or find a good job in later years. Addicted, in the course of time, to carnal desires and material pleasures, they come to renounce their ideals, any criticism of which they could not once endure, and fall into the captivity of low desires and interests. Once they have got into such a perilous state, they can no longer recover unless a heavenly hand comes to their aid, and are fettered by what they were once furious about. They become so indifferent to their previous ideals that they feel offended by the criticism of either their own conscience or somebody else, for their abuses even in their jobs or responsibilities.

From then on, they use all their abilities to maintain their posts and win the favour of their superiors, things which humiliate a man, and become more and more degraded. If they show a capacity to be promoted, they will no longer think of anything other than getting promotion even if at the cost of losing all their honour and dignity, and doing things contrary to the dictates of their conscience and faith. They will bow down before every person from whom they anticipate benefit, and display so weak a character that they may speak excessively ill of one whom they praised to the skies a day before.

The show and flattery reciprocated between them and their like are so demeaning to their already worn-out character that we can no longer expect of them any good or virtue. More pathetically, they develop the mental or spiritual 'disease' that although they have already lost their sensitivity and the ability to think and decide properly, and are completely devoid of insight and wisdom, yet they regard themselves still as ones who think better than others, who make the best judgements and do the most useful things.

And indeed it is very difficult to remind them of, or warn them against, their faults. Since the selfish souls such as those usually develop hatred and rancour against those who show them their faults, and tend to regard themselves as always right, they never like to take advice from anybody else.

Almost everyone naturally has a weakness for some things and it comes out under the appropriate circumstances. However, it is always possible to save people from drowning in the swamp of their weaknesses. If we are able to implant in the young firm belief, pure and sound thoughts, a strong feeling of altruism and an inextinguishable feeling of love of nation and country; if we enable them to come together around a sacred cause to which they should be made to dedicate themselves; if we bring them to prefer such values as honour and dignity over passing pleasures; and if we inculcate in them the duty of loyalty to the country and working for its good, and convince them that it is an unforgivable ingratitude to the blessing of time to be occupied with anything other than serving the nation and country in accordance with that sacred cause – if we are able to do all this, then the young will maintain their essential identity against mental and spiritual corruption. Otherwise, we will witness each day a star disappear from the sky of our hopes because of spiritual diseases such as love of position, attachment to life, fame-seeking and addiction to material pleasures, and we will be bowed down by disappointment and loss of hope.

FOR THE CONQUEST AND DOMINION OF HEARTS

Over the last few centuries mankind have suffered hardships after hardships, travelling around pits of 'death'. Their struggles for deliverance and relief have all resulted in new calamities. During this dark period, rather than the established governments formally in power, it is the greed and passions of individuals, classes, holding companies and mafias that have controlled communities. It hardly needs saying that in this circumstance, the only criterion by which people and things are evaluated is money, buying power.

It is natural, in a period when standards have changed so completely, that people should be esteemed for their wealth, the make of car they use and the sort of house they live in. It is natural because material and financial resources or potentials have been given precedence over human virtues like knowledge, good morals, sound thinking and civility. Wealth may indeed be valued when put under the command of knowledge, intellect, courage, honour and devotion to the service of others, but when valued for itself or, worse, when united with greed, it can be a means of brutality.

If the members of a society make the foundation of their lives the gratification of animal desires, and their purpose becoming or being rich at all costs – rather than being honest, industrious and competent, then the selfish, the ignorant and the cunning people come to dominate in that society. This means the exclusion of moral values and human virtues and therefore of those who combine efficiency with personal integrity – precisely the ones who could be useful to the society.

Compared with previous centuries, mankind today may well be wealthier and enjoying more of the conveniences and comforts of life. However, it is also true that they are trapped in greed, infatuations, addictions, needs and fantasies much more than in any previous age. The more they gratify their animal appetites, the more crazed they become to gratify those appetites still more; the more they drink, the more thirsty they are; the more they eat, the more hungry they are. They enter into bad speculations to feed their avarice to earn ever more and more and sell their spirits to the devil in return for the most banal advantages, thus breaking with true human values a little more each day.

Modern man, who spends his energies in pursuit of transient material advantages, is wasting himself and all the nobler, truly human feelings in the depths of his being. It is no longer possible to find among his resources either the serenity that comes from belief, or the tolerance and depth of spirit enabled by knowledge of God, or the traces of love and spiritual joys. This is so because he weighs everything on the scales of material advantage, immediate comfort and the gratification of bodily appetites, and thinks about only how he can increase his profit or what he will buy and sell, and where and how he will amuse himself. If he is unable to satisfy his appetites through lawful means, he rarely hesitates to resort to unlawful means, however degraded and degrading.

In order to be delivered from the suffocating world of unbelief and egocentricity, from shuttling aimlessly between the false modern concepts of thought, action and life, man should strive to re-discover the true human values that lie in the depths of his being. To escape the various stresses and afflictions in the psychological, spiritual and intellectual dimensions of personal life, and the strains and conflicts in collective affairs within and between nations, he should re-consider the worth of believing, loving, moral values, metaphysical thinking and spiritual training.

Believing means knowing the truth to be true, what and how it is, and loving means putting that knowledge into effect in one's life. Those who do not believe and love are merely physical entities without true life, like mechanically animated corpses. Belief is a most important source of action and a way to embrace the whole creation in spirit, while love is the most essential element of true human thought and a transcendental dimension of it. For this reason, those who are on the way of building the happy world of the future on the foundations of spiritual and moral values, should first arrive at the altar of belief, then ascend to the pulpit of love, and only then preach their message of belief and love to all others. In seeking to achieve their aims, they should never forget that their influence depends on morality and virtuousness.

Morality is the essence of religion and a most fundamental portion of the Divine Message. If being virtuous and having good morals is to be heroic – and it is – the greatest heroes are, first, the Prophets and, after them, those who follow them in sincerity and devotion. A true Muslim is the one who practises a truly universal, therefore Muslim, morality. Anyone of sense and insight can see that the Qur'an and the *Sunnah* – the way or example of the Prophet, upon him be peace and blessings – are sets of moral principles. The Prophet, who is the greatest embodiment of morals, said: *Islam consists in good morals; I have been sent to perfect and complete good morals.* The Muslim Community have always been the representatives of good morality and it must be so since it is only through morality and virtuousness that this Community can attain eternity. Islamic metaphysics is a means to reach the highest point in morality.

Metaphysical thought is the effort of the intellect to embrace creation as a whole and perceive it with all its dimensions, visible and unvisible. Without this effort of the intellect or spirit, everything breaks up into lifeless fragments. For this reason, the failure of metaphysical thought implies the death of the intellect. All the great civilizations have developed and come into being in the arms of metaphysical thought. Metaphysical thought is human intellect or spirit trying to embrace the whole of creation and comprehend it from within and outside; those who see metaphysics and physics (and other sciences) as conflicting disciplines, are not aware that they are seeing a river and the source where it originates as contradictory.

Another dimension of metaphysics is the perception of creation through love. In this context, love is identical with perceiving the whole of the universe with whatever is happening in it as a continuous interconnected flux and loving it. Those who have been able to find this true love pursue neither wealth nor fame; rather, they find peace in the flames of their love and see the face of their beloved amid the ashes of their own existence burnt away. In other words, they are on an uninterrupted journey from the valleys of 'self-annihilation in the existence of God' to the heights of 'attainment to permanence through permanence of God'. This attainment can come through strict spiritual training.

Spiritual training means directing man to the purpose of his creation. Through awareness of the ultimate purpose of this worldly existence, a man can be freed from bodily pressures and realize a journey into his very essence.

We are obliged to change the viewpoint and aspirations of modern man who, having lost his spiritual dynamics and broken with his essential identity, is the victim of his own self. We are hopeful that if we reinforce our will and resolve through regular worship and control it through continual self-ciriticsm, Almighty God will not deny his help in making us successful in this blessed mission. It is our duty to sow the seeds now for the brighter earth of the future, and we leave to God Himself, if He wills, to grow each of them into fruitful trees.

We are fully convinced that, as a result of conscious efforts, this corrupt world will give birth to a new one where belief and worship will carry to every place the fragrances of peace, security and love. We are also convinced that future generations will aim at, and be favoured by, the ecstasies of an overflowing love, far beyond aspirations fo money or fame or high appointments. This love will originate in conquering hearts and, in return, will be recompensed with the dominion of hearts.

MAN IN THE 'SPIRAL' OF THOUGHTS

Man is a being shaped in mind and spirit, and in character, in accordance with the view of things and the world that he has acquired after years of thinking and consideration.

Thought, intention and ambition are of the same importance in the development of a man's potentialities as the earth, air, rain and sun are in germination and growth of seeds under the soil. Intention and thought have a primary influence upon the formation of a man's morals and character. Sound minds and character develop from pure thoughts and intentions.

Thought is a seed, from which the tree of personality grows. Manners are flowers of this tree and joys and sorrows its fruits. The one who looks upon the bright side of the world thinks of good things, and the one who thinks of good things germinates in his soul the seeds of virtues and beauties, and thereby lives in the gardens he has formed in his bosom. Contrary to this, the pessimistic souls who are critical of everything and look upon their environment through the holes of their dark world, can never discern what is good and beautiful in it, nor can they truly enjoy their lives. Even if they were admitted in Paradise, they would again sing the praises of Hell and pour out their grievances to the angels of Hell, and, therefore, they always live in the pit of regrets and complaints.

Man, being the Creator's vicegerent on earth, has been created so that he should rule over the whole creation. In order to be able to carry out this significant mission, he has been endowed with great potentialities. Through systematic thinking and deepening in spiritual life, he will develop those potentialities and acquire a sublime character and personality. Pessimism and evil thoughts will, by contrast, cause him to develop an evil character, or, if, as a third alternative, he does not build his personality by developing his potentialities in accordance with the Commandments of his Creator, he will rot away, with nothing positive to give his community.

The gardens which a man builds in his soul through pure thoughts and intentions will, in the course of time, flourish so as to surround the whole world and spread the perfumes of happiness to everybody. Evil thoughts and intentions, by contrast, offer everyone 'blood, pus and filth'. In fact, man carries in his being the potentialities of being either a 'monster' or an 'angel'. In this realm of trial, he may rise to the 'highest of the high', as he may fall to the 'lowest of the low'. So, the one who uses his will-power, by reliance on God, in accordance with the demands of the Divine Will, will attain to the highest of the ranks by God's leave and help, while those who make themselves devoid of this support will regret and wail over their pitiful ends.

Although it is always questionable what part man's free will has in his accomplishments, all his duties and responsibilities are, nevertheless, based on this 'fine thread'. By seeing his strength and richness as innate impotence and poverty, by relying therefore upon God's Power and Riches and submitting his will to the Divine Will, a man can discipline himself and direct his thoughts and feelings to lofty ideals to gain eternity for them and so build his character and personality. Without being discouraged in the face of any set-backs, and without neglecting to consider again and again the prevailing circumstances, he uses his free-will as a key to discover the traps laid for him by his material, carnal self and eliminates them from his way to eternity. He also analyses his inner world continuously without being tired, and finally succeeds in realizing the mysteries of selfhood. This enables him to develop all his potentialities to virtues and beauties, and at last, as gold is obtained after tons of earth have been sifted in large cauldrons, and many other processes, he may become an ideal of humanity.

Whoever sincerely intends to become a true 'human being' and strives in this way for a whole lifetime, will one day attain his ideal and discover his real essence. The one who pursues something, usually attains it; a 'door' is opened to the one who knocks at it persistently. This is a Divine law, according to which one can be elevated to the rank of humanity through pure intentions, systematic thinking, unshakeable resolution and uninterrupted strife. Man is sent to the world equipped with the potentialities to obtain these means, and is promised help and support in his efforts to rise 'upwards'. Therefore, what is left to him to do is to use his free-will in accordance with his Creator's Commandments and attain that rank through upward movements.

HOPE

We are on the threshold of great and far-reaching changes. The community is writhing in the birth-pangs of the new time that is approaching. It is no wonder that the people are fearful, anxious, sometimes hopeless, about their future. For they have been so long abandoned in doubts and paradoxes that their imaginations are barren, their hearts and minds sick and enfeebled.

With their spirits so broken, their future so dark and undefined, it is no wonder at all that their distress has led them over the edge of despair. They long for some relief, some strength to hold themselves up and stop their legs from giving way. They long for a heroic figure to give them vigour and purpose, a message of hope.

Hope is a condition of mind connected, above all, with belief. Those who believe have hope, and their degree of hope is directly proportional to their degree of belief. It is because of this that certain effects of strong belief can strike some people as miracles. And those who do not experience belief on this level therefore consider such hope and belief in others as something quite out of the ordinary.

Despair and pessimism do not arise in the mind and spirit of one who has chosen well what he believes in and, believing, has set his whole heart upon that belief.

An individual develops by means of hope. Likewise, a community gains vitality and sets about becoming prosperous by means of hope. Just as an individual who has lost all hope cannot be regarded as truly alive, so too a community devoid of hope is disabled, paralysed.

Hope consists of a man finding his spirit and seeing the potentiality that lies within it. Perceiving that, he comes into contact with the All-Powerful and thereby obtains a power that can overcome everything. It is by that power that a particle becomes a sun, a drop of water becomes an ocean, and by it too a man's spirit becomes the breath of the universe.

The Prophet Adam, upon him be peace, when he realized he had erred, felt distressed and hopeless. But he shook off the hopelessness and revived when he said: 'I wronged myself.' Satan on the other hand faltered irrecoverably and sinks forever in the void of his despair.

All courageous men who set out with the torch of hope in their hearts have weathered storms and battled against odds that once seemed impossible. In some of them, hope is like the Ark of the Prophet Noah, upon him be peace, which carried its passengers to safety and survival through mountain-like waves. Hope changes the hearts of some others into gardens of Iram, so lively and luxuriant. Still others are so hopeful as to transmute Yathrib, a town of pagans, to Madina, the city of belief, love, and civilization.

Hope and resolution inspiring the heart of a Berber slave led him to give to the rocks of Gibraltar their name, whereby he is always remembered. Through hope, another young commander, Mehmed the Conqueror, transformed himself into lightning and cut a bright change through the course of history. He attained heights few have achieved since. Such individuals, so resolved and so filled with hope, have risen to become beloved in the sight of Truth and, to their people, are like a vivid flag, an emblem of what is possible.

Even at a time when the people are cowed down in their humiliation, their pride wounded or broken, an individual who has gained faith and hope can challenge the whole order of the world as it is. He continues in his struggle even if he suffers setbacks. And as he survives through whatever disasters befall and persists in his purpose, so he brings to life those whose spirits had been all but dead before.

It is by means of hope that journeys are undertaken, and rivers of blood and pain are crossed. Only those are defeated who fail in the realm of hope. Many are those who set out, proud of their accomplishments, and then find themselves detained or diverted halfway, because of the weakness of their faith and hope. A little earthquake, a storm or flood, takes their will and resolution away. As for those who begin in hope and then, after some setback, become bogged down in despair, their condition is truly heart-breaking. But it is in fact impossible for those unable to see the truth to do otherwise when their purposes are not realized. For those who set their hearts upon wealth and position, though always mightily cheered by transient successes, are certain, sooner or later, to be utterly disappointed.

The daytime for one who has enduring hope is as colourful as the garden of Paradise, for his heart is set upon a brightness as unfailing as the sun. His night is no less luminous. Since people of such calibre are never in the dark, the sun is always shining even when it does not appear. Those with enduring hope are rooted as solidly as great, ancient trees which neither hail or snow or freezing blizzard can cause to wither or deter from bearing fruit. Souls with hope of this quality, who have dedicated themselves to eternity, are never barren; rather, they are, in every season, fruitful, provided, ready to do what it is necessary to do.

What we need more than food, water or air, is patient, determined guides who resist corruption and hardships and never become daunted. We can derive little benefit from those who start this journey on a whim and abandon it in despair when they do not quickly attain what they are looking for, and become engaged in disputes with the Creator. The wheel of Destiny will never turn according to their corrupted way of thinking and their misguided calculations.

Now, as many buds of hope begin to appear, multitudes of seeds are waiting under the soil for the first sign of spring: may God give hope to the despairing.

COMPASSION

Compassion is the beginning of being; without it everything is chaos. Everything has come into existence through compassion and by compassion it continues to exist in harmony. The earth was put in order by messages coming from the other side of the heavens. Everything from the macrocosm to the microcosm has achieved an extraordinary harmony thanks to compassion.

All aspects of this life are a rehearsal for the afterlife and every creature is engaged in action to this end. In every struggle, order is evident; in every achievement, compassion is present. It is not possible that this effusion of compassion should go unnoticed.

Clouds hover above our heads on wings of compassion, from the centre of which rain comes down to our aid. Lightning and thunder bring us good tidings of rain with an uproar from the secret domain of compassion. The whole universe, in every particle of its being, ceaselessly sings the praises of the All-Compassionate. All creatures together extol compassion with voices peculiar to each.

Consider the worm. It is in much need of compassion being under foot, but itself displays compassion. Affectionate soil enfolds it; in turn it deposits thousands of eggs in each handful of the earth. The soil through this operation is aerated, swells, and reaches a state propitious to the sowing of seeds. While the soil is a means of compassion for worms, worms are a mercy for the soil. Words fail us to describe such careless ones who burn grass and roots to obtain manure. Poor man! He is unaware of being merciless to both soil and worms. Consider the bee approaching flowers, or the silkworm burying itself in its cocoon! What difficulties do they not encounter to take part in the symphony of compassion. Is it possible for us not to notice the pains those creatures suffer in order to provide man with honey and silk?

That is not all. Have you ever considered how heroic the chicken is that allows its head to be bitten off by a dog in order to save its young, and how praiseworthy the wolf is which, forgetting about its own hunger, offers its young the food it has found?

Everything speaks of compassion and promises compassion. Because of this, the universe can be considered a symphony of compassion. All kinds of voices proclaim compassion so that it is impossible not to be aware of it, and impossible not to feel the wide mercy encircling everything. How unfortunate are the souls who do not perceive this.

Man has a responsibility to show compassion to all living beings as a requirement of being human. The more he displays compassion, the more exalted he becomes, while the more he resorts to wrongdoing, oppression and cruelty, the more he is disgraced and humiliated, becoming a shame to humanity.

We hear from the Prophet of Truth that a prostitute went to Paradise because, out of compassion, she gave water to a poor dog dying of thirst, whilst another woman was condemned to the torments of Hell because she left a cat to die of hunger.

Mercy begets mercy. If one is compassionate on earth, then many good tidings come from heaven. Having perceived this secret, our ancestors founded a great many homes of compassion everywhere including foundations for protecting and feeding animals. A man of compassion was so deeply touched by a bird with broken legs, and a stork with damaged wings, that he established a sanctuary for injured birds; this kind of behaviour was entirely usual with Ottoman Turks.

We ought to be as compassionate to human beings as our ancestors were to animals. Alas! Just as we have not been compassionate to ourselves, so too we have ruined the next generation by showing complete indifference and pitilessness to the earth. We have actually caused the deterioration of the environment, in which it is ever more difficult to live.

We should point out, however, that abuse of the feeling of compassion can be harmful or even more harmful than being devoid of compassion altogether.

Oxygen and hydrogen, when mixed in the proper ratio, form one of the most vital of substances. On the other hand, when this ratio changes, each element resumes its original combustible identity. Likewise, it is of great importance to apportion the amount of compassion and to know who deserves it. *Compassion for a wolf sharpens its appetite, and not being content with what it receives, it demands even more.* Compassion for a rebel makes him much more aggressive, encouraging him to offend against others. It is not fitting to have compassion for the one who takes pleasure in poisoning like a snake; compassion for such a one means leaving the administration of the world to cobras.

Compassion for a bloodstained, bloodthirsty one is tyranny of the most terrible kind to all the oppressed and wronged people. Such an attitude is like being neglectful of the rights of lambs out of compassion for the wolves; it causes the whole of creation to sigh and moan, however much it might please the wolves.

LOVE

Love is the most essential element in every being, and it is a most radiant light and a great power which can resist and overcome every force. Love elevates every soul which absorbs it, and prepares it for the journey to eternity. A soul which has been able to make contact with eternity through love, exerts himself to implant in all other souls what he gets from eternity. He dedicates his life to this sacred duty, for the sake of which he endures every kind of hardship to the end, and just as he pronounces 'love' in his last breath, he also breathes 'love' while being raised on the Day of Judgement.

A soul without love is impossible to be elevated to the horizon of human perfection. Even if he lived hundreds of years, he could not make any advances on the path to perfection. Those who are deprived of love, since being entangled in the nets of selfishness, are unable to love anybody else and die unaware of love which is deeply implanted in the very being of existence.

A child is received with love when he is born, and grows up in a warm atmosphere composed of affectionate, loving souls. Even if he may not enjoy the same love in the same degree in later phases of his life, he always longs for it and pursues it throughout his life.

There are impressions of love on the face of the sun, water evaporates high towards those impressions, and after it has been condensed in drops high above, the drops come down joyfully onto the earth on the wings of love. Then, thousands of kinds of flowers burst through love and offer smiles to their surroundings. Dew drops on leaves glitter with love, and twinkle with amusement. Sheep and lambs bleat and skip about with love, and birds and chicks chirp with love and form choruses of love.

Each being takes part in the grand orchestra of love the universe with its own particular symphony and tries to demonstrate, by free will or through its disposition, an aspect of the deep love in existence.

Love is implanted in a man's soul so deeply that many people leave their home for its sake, many families are ruined and, in every corner, a Majnun groans with the love and longing for a Layla. As for those who have not been able to uncover the love inherent in their being regard such kinds of manifestations of love as madness!

Altruism is an exalted human feeling, and what generates it is love. Whoever has the greatest share in this love is the greatest hero of humanity who has been able to uproot any feelings of hatred and rancour in himself. Such heroes of love continue to live even atfer their death. These lofty souls, who, by kindling each day a new torch of love in their inner world and making their hearts a source of love and altruism, were welcomed and loved by people, got the right of living eternally from such an Exalted Court that, let alone death, even Doomsday will not be able to remove their traces.

A mother who can die for her child's sake is a heroine of affection; an individual who dedicates his life to his nation and country is a self-sacrificing member of his community, and a man who lives and sacrifices himself for humanity is a monument of immortality who deserves to be enthroned in hearts. For them, love is a weapon with which to overcome every obstacle, and a key to open every door. Those who possess such a weapon and key will sooner or later open the gates to all parts of the world and spread everywhere the fragrance of peace from the 'censers' of love in their hands.

The most direct way leading to the hearts of people is the way of love. This way is the way of the Prophets. Those who follow it are not rejected; even if they are rejected by one or two people, they are welcomed by thousands. Once they are welcomed through love, nothing can prevent them from attaining their object.

How happy and prosperous are those who follow the guidance of love. How unfortunate, on the other hand, are those who, unaware of the love deeply innate in their souls, lead a 'deaf and dumb' life!

O God, Most Exalted! Today when hatred and rancour have invaded everywhere like layers of darkness, we take refuge in Your infinite Love and entreat at Your door that You may fill the hearts of Your mischievous, pitiless slaves with love and human feelings!

CHILAH

Chilah – great suffering, trouble and hardships experienced by the traveller on the road of virtue, so as to become 'cooked' and mature, and to raise his people to spiritual and material perfection.

Chilah is inevitable in the pursuit of sublime aims and for the realization of good results. The traveller on the road of truth purifies himself of sins through suffering and by such refinement arrives at his very self. It is impossible to speak of perfection or spiritual wholeness where *chilah* has not been experienced.

Chilah is suffering with which the man of truth becomes entangled at every turn. By means of it, long ways no longer seem monotonous, life becomes illumined, and the man feels pleasure in that awareness. Life without *chilah* is wearying and dreary, and poor travellers on such ways are unfortunate and tired of living.

The spirit reaches perfection through suffering. The heart flourishes through it. Spirits who have not undergone hardship are coarse, and hearts not ripened by *chilah* are lacking in colour and vigour.

Suffering enhances the value of labour. Gains without suffering are, like possessions got by inheritance, obtained without labour and spent without grief. Only such things as are earned with great suffering are worthy that souls be sacrificed to preserve them.

If a nation or civilization has been founded through the guidance of great men who have suffered and endured, it will be healthy and stable. If, on the contrary, it has come into existence and flourished by people who never shed tears, never felt pains, never groaned, it will be unfortunate and liable to disintegration. Human beings have attained self-realization and self-consciousness at times in the compassionate, life-sustaining arms of men who have suffered, and at times under the tyranny of oppressive despots. But they have only experienced true felicity under the guidance of great men who have suffered and lived good lives.

The Prophet Abraham, upon him be peace, the man of suffering, conveyed his message throughout the region of the world now called the Middle East, and risked his life when Nimrod threw him into the fiery furnace. The Prophet Moses, upon him be peace, travelled between Egypt and Sinai many times to revive a community that had become spiritually degenerate. The Prophet Jesus, upon him be peace, preached his message not caring for the dangers surrounding him, and raised a community sunk in worldliness to spiritual realization, as if saying: *Even if you go so far as to stab me with a dagger, my friend, I shall never forsake you.* Finally, the Seal of the Prophets, Muhammad, upon him be peace and God's blessings, lived the whole of his life seeking the happiness of others, and through great suffering overcame innumerable calamities.

The fact is that those who have followed the men of great stature, who have experienced sufferings, have never been deceived or disappointed.

Those sincere guides, pure in essence, with illumined hearts, and of awe-inspiring nobility, endured many hardships. We have a great need and yearning for such guides in these days when our horizons are darkened and we have been submerged under a thousand difficulties.

Every golden age has come about because men suffered and endured for it, only to be damaged and destroyed at the hands of inexperienced persons who had suffered nothing at all. These careless, callow men completely neglected their inner worlds because of their subjection to their own carnal desires, and they are bound for the pits of Hell.

It was such careless, inexperienced souls who drowned in blood the period after the Time of Happiness, the lifetime of the Prophet Muhammad, upon him be peace and God's blessings. In subsequent periods too, gangs of the same kind plotted great conspiracies. They never suffered hunger or thirst, nor were exiled from their homes or homelands, nor exposed to hardship for any length of time. It is vain to expect any sacrifices from such souls who, never knowing distress, have spent their lives in material luxury and comfort. Sacrifice begins with resisting the low desires of the carnal self, and gains perfection through forgetting one's own happiness for the sake of the community.

O you, my carnal self, who know no suffering and have no liking for perseverance! O you, my carnal self, who are addicted to ease and comfort, who would like to consume here in this world the bounties and pleasures belonging to the next! O you, my carnal self, who deem no one but yourself the perfect man, whilst being wholly ignorant of the way to perfection! O you, my carnal self, who bring disgrace on yourself with the selfish thought – 'What does it matter if there are clouds over the hill, so long as we have sunshine here?' I do not know whether I shall be able to convince you, my carnal self, of how uplifting suffering is, and how deadly a poison the fondness for comfort.

THE DECLINE OF SPIRITUAL ENERGY

We used to have a magnificent civilization founded on faith, resolution, altruism and valour. The dark world of Europe's Middle Ages was illumined and revitalized by the learning, faith, compassion and love with which our ancestors inspired it. The era of illumination which began with the coming of our Prophet lasted for centuries. Then, we began to lose the dynamism of our civilization, to collapse. As a result, we came to regard the enemy as more powerful than ourselves. Our power of will and strength of spirit were paralysed. We sought excuses for our defeats, and considered the enemy invincible. The people, in consequence, lost their hope and resolve.

For many centuries we have deceived ourselves into believing our enemies irresistible, singing the praises of their military superiority. On occasions, we have even accused our ancestors of failing to match the technical advances of our opponents and have spoken ill of them. At other times, we have moaned that the enemy is cruel and pitiless. What we have not done is to criticize ourselves and honestly evaluate our own attitudes. In doing so, we have inflicted further heavy blows to the hope and resolve of the people. It will remain impossible to establish the real reasons for our collapse, impossible to achieve a true revival as long as we continue to ascribe our defeats only to the military or technical superiority of the enemy and the superior number of their mechanized troops.

So ask yourselves, and then tell me, have you actually fulfilled your obligations? Have you been able to pursue the right way in your activities? Do you have enough will-power and resistance to overcome the obstacles that you face? Are your thoughts and actions in conformity with your beliefs? Have you been able to keep clear of such sinister motivating forces as hatred, malice and vengeance? And your plans and projects – are they carefully, accurately and appropriately thought out?

Only those afflicted with paralysis of will-power and spirit are so blind to their own faults that they busy themselves in finding fault with others. Such poor souls will never be able to perceive the truth, nor make a spiritual recovery, unless they admit that they are themselves fallible.

Every defeat and decline from greatness arises, first of all, from spiritual bankruptcy, and it will continue until there is spiritual recovery. What is most ominous for the well-being of the community is that the spiritually bankrupt individuals do not hold themselves responsible for the decay of the social order, and persist in laying the blame for it on others.

For God's sake, stop blaming others, and allow yourself to carry a little of the blame. Be self-critical, at least a little. If indeed you are on the right way, if indeed your hearts are set on the service of the truth, and fully alert to your responsibilities, then no one will be able to do you any harm. Remember that only by the Will of God does harm or good come to anyone. Remember that the way has always been paved by Destiny for those pure, loving souls who are determined to serve and support the truth.

How often has a small, resolute and persevering band, devoted to God's way, overcome by God's leave, a more numerous host. Many devout, godly persons have spent their whole lives in the way of God, and not quailed in front of whatever has befallen them. They have neither been weakened, nor brought low. They are the fortunate ones who are welcomed by the angels, and it is they who will be commemorated by succeeding generations.

GENERATIONS WITH NO IDEALS

It is possible for a people to remain active only if they are given lofty ideals. When they are left with no ideals or aims, they become reduced to the condition of animated corpses showing no signs of distinctively human life. All the living things in nature including grass and trees continue to flourish, blossom and yield fruit so long as they remain alive. Man, too lives and continues to exist through his ideals, actions and struggles. Just as an inactive organ becomes atrophied, and a tool which is not in use becomes rusty, so idle generations will eventually waste away because they lack ideals and aims.

A society gains dynamic permanence so long as it remains faithful to the spiritual values upon which it was founded. As soon as it breaks with the cycle of renewal, it immediately begins to decompose inwardly and eventually comes to utter destruction. For this reason, a widespread effort is necessary to preserve the high ideals and sacred principles around which all individuals can unite.

It must be the foremost duty of those leaders upon whom the people have set their hopes to equip the coming generations with lofty ideals, leading them to the fountain of the 'water of life'. Such careless generations as have no aims or ideals in life will at first smoulder inwardly, and then, bursting into flames, will inevitably be led to complete destruction.

We are an unfortunate people who have several times been exposed to the most horrible calamities in recent centuries. During this period full of disappointments, friends have usually shown disloyalty and enemies have never tired of betraying us. The spiritual roots of the society have repeatedly been attacked and the mass of people frequently subjected to assaults from both inside and outside, and the whole nation has been shaken time after time. If a helping hand had not been given to us each time we were exposed to such calamities, we would have been thrown into one of those infernal pits and completely destroyed.

It is not necessary to relate what may happen in the future, and it is also not necessary to drive sensitive minds to despair by depicting corruption. Instead, we must show the people how to renew themselves. We must equip the younger generations, who will shoulder the responsibility for shaping the future, with lofty aims and high ideals.

This high duty must be undertaken by all institutions, from schools to places of worship, and it must be carried out by enlightened souls. Those who are able to combine the operations of head and heart are the only ones capable of doing it. The real guide and teacher is he who first experiences the truth in his own heart, then pours out the fire of his inspiration to ignite the hearts of his listeners. People unable to derive inspiration from the Divine Light coming from all around the universe are incapable of leading the people to the realization of true humanity. Likewise, those who have yielded to doubts have nothing to give their students. At most, such guides can only console the people with epics and recitals from the past, empty ceremonies, and folklore performed in the name of religion. They spend their time in relating the good deeds and accomplishments of others, which can neither arouse enthusiasm nor give uplifting thoughts to the minds nor empower the will of their listeners.

To console oneself with re-telling the heroic deeds of others indicates a psychological weakness peculiar to the impotent, who have failed to discharge their responsibilities to the society. In a community consisting of such people, the spirit of adventure is replaced by excessive praise of the past and songs of victories and heroism. Religious thought and obligations are reduced to formalities and festivals, which are performed by people devoid of zeal and vigour. Again, in such a community, the ways to the pious life are blocked by debased practices and shallow thoughts, and by barren minds who content themselves with the narration of the wonderful accomplishments of others.

Of course, we should certainly commemorate the saints of our past with deep emotion and celebrate the victories of our heroic ancestors with enthusiasm. But we should not think this is all we are obliged to do, just consoling ourselves with tombs and epitaphs.

Heroism is something to be expressed in songs only after it has been proven on the battlefields; for it is possible to be a soldier of God by rising to eternity upon the wings of love and sacrifice. Faith has to be proved by confessing sincerely that religious obligations are the aim of life and by performing these obligations with the utmost care and devotion.

Each scene from the past is valuable and sacred only so long as it stimulates and enthuses us, and provides us with knowledge and experience for doing something today. Otherwise it is a complete deception, since no success or victory from the past can come to help us in our current struggle.

Today, our duty is to offer humanity a new message composed of vivid scenes from the past together with understanding of the needs of the present.

ATTACHMENT TO LIFE

Attachment to this life leads to the diminishing of human faculties, to inward decay until man's spirit falls into a most wretched state. The enjoyment of luxurious living paralyses such feelings as exalt man, and is a blow to resolution and will-power. Clinging to luxuries is an evil that corrupts the individual, and is a great obstacle to the maintenance of a harmonious society. Until the individual frees himself from this evil, and the society clears away this obstacle, the whole community will remain morally paralysed and the country will eventually be filled with poorhouses.

Enjoyment of a luxurious life-style means living mainly for pleasure, and has corrupted and led astray every people it has taken hold of, and finally ruined them. Ancient nations and civilizations, whose existence we only know about from the pages of history, all wasted away because of luxury and attachment to easy living. Their destruction has caused those who came after them to feel nothing but regret.

There is Pompeii with its lessons, and ancient Egypt, Rome, al-Andalus (Islamic Spain) and the Ottoman Empire. All of these civilizations were completely ruined by similar calamities caused by a similar destiny. They became infatuated with the fatal charms of pleasure, then were brought to ruin.

If only we had been able to remember and learn the terrible lessons of the past, then we should have been better prepared.

Alas! Where are those with the right kind of perception, and the necessary spiritual knowledge? How many people have taken warning from events which have occurred time after time in their past?

Therefore, history repeats itself. Indulgence, extravagance and spiritual decadence continue to cause new calamities, so that once great nations which founded civilizations decayed into silence. Decay was inevitable for them, because they ignored the truth and betrayed their ideals. God opened to them many benefits in this life but, as a result of their sins, they only entered deeper into their sins thereby, until, little by little, they were drowned in perdition. They desired only to live at their ease and sought from life only the utmost pleasure. They could not be allowed to continue living with such indifference and insensitivity, so heaven burst open with rage and emptied itself upon them, and the earth carried to them all its hatred and anger.

How great a warning is the scene of Pompeii, which perished with its disgusting public baths and luxurious palaces, immersed in indeceny and obscenity! If only those who conveyed the new spirit to al-Andalus had known of and understood this warning and taken a lesson from it! What of the later Ottoman rulers who might have discerned their own impending doom from the tragic fate of Egypt, Rome and al-Andalus?

If only they had given up covering the walls and ceilings of their palaces with gold, spending their nights in feather beds, and swaggering about in bright uniforms and satin cloths! If only they had returned to the frontiers at the head of their armies! Alas, that they did not. When the emperor restricts himself to the palace, abandoning the imperial army, the administrative staff of the state begin to intrigue against one another. Ease and comfort, in which the statesmen are thoroughly immersed, finally infect the army and rot it. The army, that training-ground of holy warriors, which had once been all-conquering in the name of God, was now inspired with low desires, and rebelled against its own administration and rulers. Such was the road to decline and fall of a great, magnificent state, which had once dominated three continents.

How tragic a defeat and how hopeless an extinction that was: *my mind becomes confused when I recall the country of Salah al-Din Ayyubi and Mehmed the Conqueror.*

Is it possible for today's unfortunate generation, who have made efforts to overcome the calamities of the past, to found the world of the future on the basis of the lessons and warnings they have learned from the past? If they do not, the same consequences of decay and destruction are inevitable for them, too. Let us hope the lesson has been learned! What a pity that, whilst in the prime of life, we have become immersed in the same filth in which those who preceded us were drowned. Preoccupied with ease and comfort, we have completely forgotten about the good people of this land. We have set out to live in this world the pleasant life promised for the Hereafter, and have been reduced to being slaves of carnal desires. Deviating from the sacred way, along which we had set out with great zeal, we have abandoned the important undertakings and duties in favour of luxury and worldly adornments. We have abandoned our duties in favour of a cheap, worldly gain.

What a pity we have deceived ourselves. We suppose this worldly life to be eternal, and because of that supposition we completely waste our life. Events in this life are no more than dreams, so quickly do they pass: it is a life without permanent foundation and flows away like a river. If we continue to deceive ourselves by singing for union with the Beloved while lying back at our ease, we shall, like the ruler of Balkh, need a sharp re-awakening: [one night in bed, this ruler, Ibrahim ibn Adham, while thinking of meeting with God, heard a noise coming from the attic. He asked: 'Who is there?' A voice answered that he was searching for his lost camel. Ibrahim ibn Adham retorted: 'A lost camel is not to be looked for in an attic.' The voice replied: 'Meeting with God is not to be looked for in a soft bed.' The effect of this incident upon Ibrahim ibn Adham led him to quit his throne.]

At a time when everyone is rushing about after wages and profits, and everything worthwhile is sacrificed to ease and comfort, we offer these thoughts in the hope of the attention of a generation prepared to forget their material and even spiritual pleasures for the sake of a higher goal.

SOME DROP OUT HALF-WAY

Dedicated to those of us whose heads have
been turned by the pleasures of this life.

I thought that each bud would grow into a flower and all of
the flowers would last forever. I thought that the rosebuds covering our lands would always remain fresh, and the crops
growing in our fields always grow abundantly! I thought that
the shoots which sprouted after the long winter would reach
eternal spring through the efforts of great men of suffering and
remain fresh forever.

I thought that the moon and the sun would always continue
to follow each other on my horizon, and that the sky of my
country would never witness an eclipse of either sun or moon.

I thought that whoever had awaited the spring for years
would not retire into hibernation when the signs of spring appeared. I thought that they would not turn back without drink-
ing the water of life after they had met Khidr.

I thought that the members of our community, who have
been taken in thousand of times, would no longer be deceived
and surrender to other deceptions by the same cheats.

I thought that each one of us who has been revived spiritually would remain active and alive, and never suffer illnesses,
and that the ethos around him would spread the scent of revival. The wooden boards upon which the dead are washed

would crack because of disuse, I thought, that things which are applied to the dead like musk and camphor would no longer be needed. I thought that spiritual death would no longer occur.

I thought this community of sincere, altrustic men, which set out to serve under the threat of death like the Apostles, would never join those who desired to crucify Jesus. I thought wealth, fame and position would not make them go astray to change their path, and that mean things would not seduce them, and they would always have the same high thoughts in their minds and the same songs on their lips. I thought they would lead their lives with the same propriety.

I thought that this army of godly men, who made a covenant with the Creator to stop the suffering of the oppressed and to silence the tyrants, would never side with the oppressors. I thought they would never belittle their past and separate from it for the sake of transient pleasures or for the sake of remaining undisturbed. I thought that devotion to our spiritual roots would become stronger and stronger, and that our ideals would never be abandoned. I believed our manners would never change. Like pure rivers flowing into seas, our lives would renew themselves. I thought paths and channels leading in different directions would unite at the point where roads lead to infinity.

I thought that the different characters would eventually form a heavenly unity like a rainbow and others would willingly join this unity.

I thought love of pleasures and fondness for comfort would never take hold of this community, and that they would always remain pure and humble. That they would never be seized by the luxury and extravagance which have eaten up previous civilizations.

I thought that the members of our community would be content with the friendship of the One, to whom they have given their hearts. I thought that they would always seek His approval without desiring to satisfy the wishes of others, that, saying 'God is enough, the rest is empty desire', they would carry on.

They think they can gain the approval of those who are their permanent enemies by changing in thought and in behaviour. Alas, they do not realize how they mortgage their spirits and blind their hearts by doing so.

They believe that they can gain weight for their words and opinions by sympathizing with their opponents. They seek to gain favour with their enemies by having painted and decorated ceilings, tablecloths with silk threads, satin bed-linen, and polished floors. They do not realize that they will only expose themselves to ridicule thereby.

They believe that lightness in their behaviour, and triviality in their thoughts and their aspirations, will cause others to love them and that they will therefore attract others to their way of thought. They do not realize that they themselves unconsciously join their enemies and lose their own identity thereby.

We are about to live a new spring. The earth is pregnant with trickles of water, seeds move with germinating life, as also do snakes with poison. We shall see who is on the side of the spring and who of winter. Who will go after bargains and who will dive deep to search for coral. Who will boast about their easy-to-lose possessions and who will go beyond themselves and the world, attaining to eternity. We all shall see. We shall see who will melt away like wax in the face of the transforming power of the world, and who can change the turning of this pitiless wheel....

Time will show which of us shall be victorious in his struggle....

STARTLING SCENES

With bewildered eyes and a heart shaking between disappointment and hope, I watch events throughout this country in particular and the world in general. I watch some who are beaten by storms like pine trees in a gale; some who collapse and are broken; some who, despite all misfortunes and against all odds, carry on, with a bold swing of the arm, sowing the seeds in season; and some who are tried and tested in the crucible of suffering and attain eternity while still on earth.

Floods come, one after the other; great tidal waves like falling towers; and mighty convulsions, also in series. I wonder at these events, preparing the ground for a new formation, a new birth: I watch and bewildered: how diamond is separated out from coal, gold from false stone, the wholesome from the rotten.

Lofty ideals are ridiculed and a whole past cursed. A dark thought pervades hearts and minds, flatters dark souls and paves the way for destructive movements. It causes rifts and troubles in the society, progressing through unimaginable falsehoods, false accusations, tricks and betrayals, it paralyses the labour of a whole nation, their very power to think. Vast regions of mankind groan under the tyranny of despotic rulers more pitiless than Nero. The struggles and services of those who would teach the nation to find again their real essence and identity are branded with being reactinoray in thought, obscurantism and the like. There are many who have as yet been unable to come to their senses, who waste their lives in self-indulgence and entertainments, run after vain luxuries. There are many who, for fear of getting into trouble, prefer to remain indifferent to what is happening around them, who bury their heads in pointless competition with one another for banal advantages. There are those who, while charged with healing the ills of the nation, have been too long habituated to preying on others, and sniff about for blood to drink, dry the nation's veins. There are those compelled to silence in the face of every disaster... I watch and wonder, in profound distress, amid enraged, embittered tears...

Although religious life is founded upon solemn sincerity and earnest, some change it into a species of folklore and their means of livelihood. I watch those who make the Qur'an into sing-songs for a living, whose revenue is the religious life sold as ceremonies: I watch all this; and I witness it, before my Lord, trembling in utmost shame.

The modern Neros commit the most blatant, outrageous atrocities in various parts of the world; among the millions of the oppressed, incalculable numbers are massacred or abandoned to hunger and thirst, slow deaths. I watch all this, and other causes of shame for modern 'civilized', 'liberated' man. I watch, and look for signs of Divine compassion through all these calamities and cruelties, doubtless pregnant with eventualities unforeseen.

I watch those who, having set their hearts on a sacred, sublime cause, nevertheless drop back half-way; who, having set out with earnest spiritual resolve to attain a destination, turn on their heels before reaching the battle-lines; who, having left to hunt stars, return with fire-flies on the points of their spears. I watch and wonder in grief.

I watch those who, despite the primordial nobility of their spirits and the sense of eternity, the yearning for it in their deepest nature, yield to animal impulses, blind to the beauties of the eternal life beckoning them with smiles but three steps ahead. I watch them crushed under the burden of those animal impulses, and I watch in pain.

I note the patience of the All-Merciful, His clemency, in His granting respite to the ignorant and unmannerly, to the unjust and cruel, even to heretics and aggressors. I note His constancy of custom in His arrest of those who in their atrocities have gone beyond the wide limits He established... I note these in full conviction and shiver.

Bewilderment hangs like a mist before my eyes; hopes and disappointments beat in my heart; I watch the events and I await their issue.

THE HORIZON OF SHAME

Many have wept at the contrast between a glorious, uplifting past and the distressing circumstances of their nation's present, at the decline of a magnificent civilization.

How many times have our people been pleased to hear the sound of the fountain of life like Ayyub (Job), upon him be peace. How many times like Jacob longing for Joseph, upon them be peace, have they been hopeful of reunion. They take the signs supporting their hopes to be the scent of Joseph's shirt coming from Egypt. In a like manner, the people are singing songs of reunion in expectation that the Time of Happiness will recur. If there had not been such signs of revival giving refreshment to our souls, we should probably have perished. The community has been able to preserve its essential nature during the dark years of destruction without breaking with its origins. This was only because of guidance coming from those who had determined to establish the future. Younger generations will never forget those enlightened persons who passed away honourably with no blemish upon their lives or characters.

Peace be upon those friends who passed away in blessed memory. Peace be upon those spirits who held the world and life to be of little value compared with their sacred cause. Peace be upon those who bade farewell without demanding any wages after they had planted the seed of truth. Peace be upon those people of noble stature who would not mind being burnt in the flames of Hell so long as they might thereby secure the faith and sound thinking of their people. Peace be upon those who spent their lives in great difficulties because of their opening up the way of struggle for succeeding generations. They all gave up the pleasures of life and lived for others. They all succeeded in avoiding everything shameful and departed from this life with honour and dignity.

Shame upon those who are unmoved by the pains and troubles of their people. Shame upon those carefree people who wander in utter indifference and neglect over the ruins of a magnificent civilization, which has gradually been destroyed. Shame upon such blind ones who live without noticing our dried-up water courses, wasted vineyards, our damaged bridges and ruined roads. Shame upon those who have reduced the meadows to wasteland and polluted the country, making land and sea uninhabitable. Shame upon those who praise ruins, but do not react against moss-covered *mihrabs* (the place where the leader of prayer stands before the congregation) and cobwebbed ceilings. Shame upon those who have not been able to make use of their opportunities, making individuals idle and institutions unproductive. Shame on those who try to exploit even the dead for their own advantage.

I feel disgraced by such betrayal and widespread shamelessness. I feel ashamed of disloyalty to my people and indifference to their destruction. I feel ashamed of my own inability to support the truth and save it from the attacks of falsehood. I feel ashamed because I did not appreciate the warnings of the past, and because I do not prefer an honourable death to a humiliating life. I feel ashamed of the injustices I have committed, and the many betrayals darkening the horizon of the country. I feel ashamed of hypocrisies, pretensions and insincerities. I feel ashamed of the hardness of my heart, my insensitivity, and the humiliation bearing heavily on my conscience. I feel ashamed because I have not given up my pleasures for the sake of my people, because I have not cried over their problems on my prayer-mat, because I have not forgotten about my self and my household and remembered their sufferings.

If only we could feel ashamed enough for our insensitivity and indifference to the spiritual misery of the community! If only we could feel ashamed enough because our people have been left in ignorance for years and our young have been pitilessly neglected! If only we could feel ashamed enough about the duties we have left unattended for years and about the multitudes of problems unattempted! If only we could feel shame enough before God – even if we do not feel ashamed before our past and future generations!

CHAOS AND BELIEF

The earth has so far witnessed many upheavals one after the other, and mankind have suffered disappointments because of these upheavals. However, as night is followed by morning and winter by spring, no upheaval has been permanent and it has been followed by a happier time.

The modern age will probably be remembered in the future as the period of the deepest convulsions and the cruelest and most destructive upheavals. I think that the earth has never witnessed craziness so widespread and great as today's. As Bernard Shaw once put it, if there are living beings on other planets resembling us, they most probably see the world as an asylum. It is true that modern man is in depressions incomparable to those witnessed in previous times and, accordingly, resembles a lunatic more than anything else, and so the world comes to resemble a land of lunatics.

Up to this age, mankind were aware of only local happenings. That is, most people knew about and were interested in the events that happened in their near environment. But today, because of the gigantic developments in telecommunication and transportation, the world has contracted into so small a place that every happening in some part of it interests everyone deeply and causes either uneasiness and anxiety or joy and the feeling of security. However, we, the people of 'the third world', have so far not been able to get relief and have lived in endless anxieties. It seems that this will continue until righteous people, who combine intellectual enlightenment with profound spirituality and great activism, seize the reins of the world.

There may be some who regard it as impossible for humankind to recover once more. However, we have never despaired of the future of mankind and, even in the most distressing periods, we have maintained our hope that mankind will one day re-discover their essential identity and build a new world for themselves. The sensitivity and awareness which the worldwide tumults begin to arouse in the consciousness of people is strengthening this hope. It is our conviction that mankind will, in a near future, find the exalted values which have been long sacrificed to some passing fancies, and re-adopt them. Among these values, belief in God, which no upheavals or even radical changes in social or intellectual arenas have ever been able to eradicate from the hearts of people, has always been, and will undoubtedly be, the foremost and most important support of mankind in reshaping the world.

New movements of religious revival are being observed in Christendom. These movements will one day find their true course and play a significant part in world-wide revival of mankind. In the Muslim world, mosques increase in number day by day and are filled particularly by young people. All this shows that, while hundreds of world-powers have become things of the past, and hundreds of rulers, like Caesar or Alexander the Great or Napoleon, are subject to being forgotten, religion shows its invincible power once more.

Some claim that belief is something no longer powerful enough to move masses, and that believing persons are narrow-minded and usually ignorant. This argument is no more than a deceit intended to hinder the spread of Islam among people. As admitted even by some sociologists, the next century will no doubt be the age of the true religion and no one can prevent the majority of mankind from reunion with their essential nature. Belief will once more defeat the forces of atheism, and no one will be able to extinguish the light which God has put in the hearts of people.

Existence took on the form of 'cosmos' after a chaotic state. The same is true for all the chaotic states in the history of mankind. Many convulsions or revolutions have finally brought about agreeable changes in the course of history. There has never been a year during which winter did not lead on to spring, and nights have always been followed by daytime. Therefore, we hope that mankind will overcome the present disrupting and reach the morning of a happy future.

Human history has never been devoid of 'heroes', who lead their communities to salvation. Among them, the Prophets and their successors whether in intellectual or spiritual or social arenas, have usually been able, despite the many obstacles put in their way and torments of every kind, to illuminate the way of their people to truth and ultimate victory. Mankind have entered upon the same way once more and will, by God's Will and Power, reach their ultimate destination.

CIVILIZATION OR CONFUSION OF CONCEPTIONS

In the past, civilization was defined as the coexistence of people who come together, whether in a city or district or a village, around humanistic thoughts and feelings and conscious of their being human. Since human beings naturally live in groups, they have, from the beginning, lived in some degree of civilization. A true civilization is based on the refinement of manners, thoughts and feelings, and the strength of human will-power. Although some tend to identify civilization with dazzling advances and innovations in sciences and technology – from trains to space-ships, from broad streets and tall buildings to dams and nuclear power stations, from telecommunication systems to electronics – all these are, as regards civilization, no more than means of an easy, luxurious life.

Modern facilities can help to 'modernize' the outward appearance of life, but that does not amount to being civilized. Civilization is an atmosphere propitious for the development of man's potentialities, and a civilized man is one who has put himself under the service of his community in particular, and humanity in general, alongwith the thoughts, feelings and abilities he has developed and refined in that atmosphere. For this reason, civilization is not to be sought in riches, luxury and a comfortable life in large, richly-furnished houses, nor in techniques and quantities of production and consumption, which are all elements of material pleasures and physical well-being. It is to be found rather in the purity of thoughts, refinement of manners and feelings, and soundness of views and judgements. Civilization lies in the spiritual 'evolution' of man and his continuous self-renewal towards true humanity and personal integrity – being the 'best pattern' of creation. In particular, it should be noted that civilization is not, as it is unfortunately understood by blind imitators of the West, a garment to buy from some shop and put on. Rather, it is a final destination reached along a rational way going through time and circumstances.

Civilization is different from modernism. While the former means the changing and renewal of man with respect to his views, way of thinking and human aspects, the latter consists in the changing of his life-style and bodily pleasures and the development of living facilities. Although this is the truth, the new generations, who have been bewildered through misuse of concepts, have first been misled in their way of thinking and then made to degenerate in belief, language, national thoughts, morals and culture. Apart from this, those Western peoples enjoying technical facilities more than others, and the so-called 'intellectuals' who have emerged among Eastern peoples, and who consider themselves civilized and the others as savage, have committed, through such mis-labelling, a grave, unforgivable sin against civilization and culture. Those peoples and 'intellectuals' should know that as civilization does not mean modernism, so being intellectual is quite different from being a school graduate. The number of true intellectuals who have not studied at a school is not less than high school or even university graduates who have not been able to free themselves from savagery. Misuse of concepts may cause long-lasting deceptions: people may, for ages, confuse white with black, justice with wrong-doing, enlightenment with ignorance, being intellectual with dark-mindedness and civilization with savagery.

The enlightenment of a community and its being freed from confusion of thoughts, expressions and convictions, requires the existence of a group of true intellectuals. However, as we have said, being intellectual should not be confused with being a school graduate. In any particular community, there may be people who have specialized in different branches of science, but the enlightenment of that community is possible – not through those who have studied physics, chemistry or biology – but through those true intellectuals who, in the awareness of the age, lead their life at the level of the spirit and have awaken to existence in soul and intellect by using their will-power in accordance with the dictates of truth. By combining the truths of sciences with the inspirations coming from beyond the visible worlds to form an inextinguishable source of light, they have truly been revived in soul and intellect, and have opened the way to the revival of their community through the messages they disseminate. Only through the efforts of those intellectuals can a true civilization come to existence.

Every new civilization is born through attempts based on a unique love and belief. It is in vain to talk about civilization where there are no such love and belief. In addition, if despotic pressures or interventions are added to the lack of love, belief and zeal, even the conquest of space and discovery of sub-atomic worlds will not be enough to found a civilization.

If the masses in a community are devoid of belief, love, zeal and the feeling of responsibility, if they live an aimless life unconscious of their true identity and unaware of the age and environment they live in, that community cannot be regarded as civilized even if it has changed thoroughly with all its institutions, and the living standards have risen considerably, and the people have all been 'modernized' in their life-style. For, as we have reiterated, civilization is an intellectual and spiritual phenomenon, nothing to do with technology, with dress and finery, with furniture and luxuries. The bloodshed, the continuance of colonialism under different names, unending massacres and conflicts, unchanging of human attitudes, unrefinement of manners, unenlightenment of intellectual life, the dominance of materialism in science and world views, all these, together with many other signs of savagery prevailing world-wide, show decisively that the 'developed' peoples of the world have not founded a true civilization, and nor have their 'developing' imitators been able to do so.

How pitiful it is that the intelligentsia of 'developing' countries have deceived their people into believing that they could be civilized through modernization of their life-style, which means absolute dependence on the West. This is, in fact, what the West has always suggested to them in order to block up the way to their true civilization. The 'Westernized' modernists in those countries have never been afraid of carrying out what has been 'inspired' to them by the West, and, through concerted assaults on the religion, language and way of thinking of their people, have achieved a hundred times more than what a hundred armies of crusaders would fail to achieve.

However, we are hopeful that the world will undoubtedly witness true civilization once more, and the signs of this civilization which will be founded on belief, love, knowledge and universal moral values, have already appeared on the horizon. It suffices for the realization of this sacred cause that the new generations who have undertaken it should go on their way with a strong belief and will-power and ever-deepening resolve.

REGRETS ABOUT SCIENCE AND TECHNOLOGY

The general atmosphere and conditions surrounding us promise greatly happiness so long as science and technology with all their facilities and fruits are devoted to the service of humanity. Nevertheless, so far we have not been able to make proper use of these extensive possibilities. The happiness of humanity has been delayed. There is some doubt and despair because nobody has taken on the responsibility for guiding humanity to eternal bliss. Such will probably continue to be the situation until those who have authority and competence come to acknowledge their true responsibility.

In the past, cities and villages used to live in an isolation that was unpleasant, disorderly and devoid of spirituality. They were frequently visited by privation and pestilence and were permeated by immoralities. Moreover, they merely observed what was going on with indifference, believing life to consist of nothing but this. Today, it is obviously impossible to live with out-of-date conceptions which have nothing to do with reality. *Continuing the old state being impossible, it means either following the new state or annihilation.* We will either reshape our world as required by science, or we shall be thrown into a pit together with the world we live in.

Some believe that doing this will reduce man to a machine, and mankind to a swarm of ants, running the world in accordance with mechanistic science. This is not true at all! Just as the past was not without science, so too, the future cannot be without it; everything in the end is connected with science. A world without some science has nothing to give to man.

It is, however, true that in some of our cities man has been reduced, human feelings have been diminished, certain human virtues together with health and ability to think have been wiped out. But it is an injustice to ascribe all this to science and technology. The fault lies rather with the scientists who avoid their responsibilities. Many worrying conditions would probably not have existed if the scientists had acquired an awareness of their social responsibility and had performed what was expected of them.

Science means comprehending what things and events tell us, and what the Divine Laws prevailing over the universe reveal to us. It means striving to understand the purpose of the Creator. Man, who has been created in order that he shall rule over all things, needs to observe, read, discern and learn about what is around him. Then, he has to seek the way of exerting his influence over events and subjecting them to himself. At this point, by the decree of the Sublime Creator, everything will submit to man, who himself will submit to God.

Science, with all its branches such as physics, chemistry, astronomy, medicine and so forth, is at the service of humanity, and every day brings new gains which may also be gifts of hope.

There is no reason for man to be afraid of science. The danger does not lie with science itself and the founding of a world in accordance with it, but rather with ignorance, and the irresponsibility of scientists.

We acknowledge that some planned acts based on knowledge may sometimes give bad results, but it is certain that ignorance and disorganization always give bad results. For this reason, instead of being opposed to the products of science and technology, it is necessary to use them so as to bring happiness to man. Herein lies the essence of the greatest problem of mankind. It is simply not possible to take measures against the space age or to remove the thought of making atomic or hydrogen bombs from the minds of some people.

Given that science might be a deadly weapon in the hands of an irresponsible minority, we should nonetheless adopt science with its products to found a civilization where man will be able to secure his happiness in this world and the next. It is vain to curse the machine and factories, because machines will continue to run and factories to operate. So too science and its products will not cease to be harmful to mankind until the men of truth assume the direction of things and events.

We must not fear science or the technology it enables, for such a fear paralyses every sort of activity. Instead, we must be fearful of the hands using it. Science in the hands of an irresponsible minority is something disastrous which could on its own change the world into hell. Having come to know only after the destruction of Hiroshima and Nagasaki that a monster of cruelty had exploited his studies of the atom, Einstein apologised in tears to his Japanese counterparts, but by then it was too late!

That calamity was neither the first nor will it be the last of its kind. Seas have been changed into sewage and poison, rivers into canals of filth, and the atmosphere into a fog of pollution by the barbarian minority, and this will continue to be so...

Mankind have never suffered harm from a weapon in the hands of angels. Whatever they have suffered has all come from deprived, ambitious souls who believe only that *might is right*. This situation will continue until mankind builds a world on the foundation of science and faith.

It is our hope that human beings will come to comprehend the nature of the world they live in before it is too late.

THE AGE OF SPEED

This age could certainly be called an age of speed. With the technology of speed, the world promises many diverse benefits to mankind. It brings prosperity, comfortable, easy living for some people; the gap between an idea and its enactment is reduced; the shrinking of distances increases the potential for rapid realization of projects (and, of course, of interventions in those projects by others); conflicts may break out more suddenly and then be more quickly reconciled. Science fiction imagines a future world where events happen at the speed of light – with, as yet, imaginary benefits and dangers. But mankind should be alert, in the here and now, to the danger that the technology of speed may not be used in the interests of truth and justice.

Speed, movement over distance in time, is as old as the universe; the sensation of speed was 'experienced' as soon as man was created and covered distances by walking. Man has ever since extended and advanced his power of movement until speed has reached its present, dizzying level and continues to increase. Man first 'enjoyed' speed through his feet, then on the back of domesticated beasts, then in carts and carriages, then bicycles and motor-driven vehicles. Today, man is on the verge of defeating, even annihilating, distances. The annihilation of distance is already a reality in the case of sound and image transmission by processes far ahead of the transportation of objects.

Speed has brought more ease and comfort, but has also had

negative consequences. Whether the positive consequences outweigh the negative ones is still an open question, one we can only answer by balancing the technological advances against real and substantial gain in human happiness and in the meaningfulness of human life.

Buses, trains, ships and planes, running on some advanced form of electrical energy, or in the further future space-craft run on some form of pure light energy, will make it possible to cover huge distances in minutes. We will, at the same time, be able to press a button and receive sounds, images, colours, even smells, from long distances. As 'time' and 'space' are effectively reduced, the earth will really become a global village.

Human conquests over time and space are, as we have noted, set to go much further, bringing with them, in addition to many facilities, numerous problems. We are bound to admire advances in scientific research, new inventions and their application – all the wonders of civilization. However, need this prevent us from asking whether the dazzling speed – attained through man's commitment to investigating every detail of the 'book of the universe' – has really served the nobler aims, those rather more important for human life than speed by itself. If, by subjugating time and space, by contracting the world into a village and reducing time costs to near zero, speed cannot reach the higher goals, does it really benefit mankind? If science, penetrating into the universe's remotest corners for knowledge of the whole of existence, made the whole world as familiar as our own neighbourhood, uncovered everything in it, making it, as it were, naked, and did not do so for the sake of the higher human values, needs and desires, would it not be a kind of ignominy to use such a science – to be familiar with the secrets of an individual or a nation, and able to expose them?

Is speed an end in itself? That is, are inventions and developments in transportation and telecommunication made just to indulge a crazy, unreflecting addiction to doing things ever faster? It is doubtful if these sophisticated means of transportation and communication have led to any great advance in human values. We wish that they had, so that we might look forward to the peaceful co-existence of the world's peoples in a world contracted to a village. But it is impossible to claim that the technologies of speed serve any such goal at present.

If we argue that speed is desired, not for its own sake, but for the service of mankind's loftier goals, can we also argue that faster cars or trains or planes really contribute to the attainment of these goals? If they do, we can aim to contract time and space still further – to the very limits of science-fictional imagination. But it is difficult to give a positive answer to that question: the present applications of speed technology are far from achieving the desired goals.

If speed is meant to save time, to get things done faster or to reach somewhere faster, but the time saved, the things done or the destinations reached, are not part of some higher aim more important than speed, then what is all the effort for? If we have no general aim for our speed technology and no specific intention to realize this aim, then all our effort and the time saved will be in vain – like streams of water flowing nowhere, or rain falling on barren ground. Today, some proponents of speed, heedless of any general aims in life, are greatly impressed by a technology that allows one to leave the earth's atmosphere in a few minutes, to carry sounds and images many thousands of kilometers almost instantaneously. They value only the speed, they evaluate only the technology, detached from its general consequences. However, speed is only a material phenomenon. Without specific goals it can be neither a foundation for progress and civilization nor a means to the realization of human values. While mankind found happiness in centuries when they travelled on foot or horseback, they have in this century, unfortunately, suffered from the most horrifying kinds of brutality despite very sophisticated technology.

Speed has never been the most urgent need of mankind. It was and is only a means to an end. A balanced view is important. Some have idolized speed and glorified technological advances, regarding these as everything; others, reacting against the uselessness of speed without purpose, have become hostile to modern mechanisms of transport or communication.

Speed should serve specific aims. It is to be welcomed and valued as long as it enables the realization of human values and human aims; as long as it brings peace and happiness and ends pangs of separation; as long as it contributes to the general harmony of the world and the solution of worldly and other-worldly problems; and as long as it advances scientific research and empowers scientific establishments. Without these benefits, speed in movement or communication is no more than a meaningless, insecure illusion.

THE HORIZON OF HOPE

With strong conviction and high hope, poised to move forward; with firm resolve, our will ready as a taut bow-string is ready; in sweet imagination of paradise-like scenes of tomorrow, whose beauty we experience in spirit – we speak of the future once more, alert to its being near. It is as if the dark clouds – clouds that have been covering our foundations built of a deep spirituality, and our shining past built of ivory and pearl, crystal and coral, and our culture woven with threads of satin and silk, and gold and silver – the dark clouds are moving away and an attractive, enchanting world is gliding across the horizon. The scenes appearing to us, as yet afar, produce such thrills of pleasure in our souls that we feel as if the happy, promised time had all but arrived.

Realities mixed with imagining, we feel we are half-way to the peaceful union of the modern with the traditional, the scientific with the religious and spiritual, the reason with the heart, the experienced with the revealed, and the military power with sense, justice and right. We are travelling toward this goal and feel as if we heard lyrical melodies that harmonized the past and the future. With the hope that the day will certainly come when souls conceive of nothing but goodness and fairness, when feelings overflow with love and compassion and eyes become more generous than clouds in pouring tears of mercy, when the soil fully awakens to life and the earth becomes as safe and comfortable as a nest, when human beings compete with spiritual beings in goodness and virtue – we try to meet in cheerful faith all the requirements of travelling to those horizons where we shall taste life once again as it should be.

We are hopeful because all the preparations made, the efforts exerted, and the hardships endured, are like melodies of the happy future world in whose warmth the past and the future will be embraced and the present time will unburden itself to its faithful, blessed friends, and we will sing joyful songs of the lost paradise regained.

We are hopeful because things begin to voice the wise purpose in their creation; the sun, the moon and stars begin to discourse about the past; worlds far beyond our own send smiles ahead to those expected happy days, and the preparations of a coming celebration are observed everywhere. Hoping to God that an adverse wind does not rise up to pull everything down; that space, this island of time, where souls, deeper in spirit than their actions, whose beliefs and actions are louder than their words, whose hearts and minds are set upon eternity, alight and depart, will be the island where mankind have been longing to dwell since the beginning of their worldly existence, the island which will transport them to eternity from its harbours and quays and platforms.

It is truly so. If we stir up things around us just a little, they will, as a part of history, begin to speak and sing the praises of the future. We may liken our moment in time to a clock waiting to be wound up. In appearance quite still or 'out of order' it is ready to work with the slight effort of winding. This moment of time too is about to move, like an athlete at the starting-pistol. Indeed, may we not say that it has already started – to be united with its roots in the past and search for new horizons in the future? Its movement is a rhythmical one directed by wisdom and promising springtimes, one after another; from it are heard sounds of profound resonance and music sublime.

The basic dynamics of this movement are belief and hope, while its future lies in Prophetic resolve to persevere without leaving room for any kind of deficiencies in reasoning or understanding or feeling. It is God, and only He, Who will produce the result, and it is an offence to Him to strike attitudes that imply that our hands determine and produce the result. If we reflect upon the present situation and the unimaginable effects of the dynamics we have from yesterday to the present, we could not help but be amazed by seeing how great rewards are given for the least of efforts. Ponder the fact that, although the values belonging to us have been unjustly chewed up between the teeth of time, still they have been able to reach the coastlines of our century and we can re-achieve them as the indispensable elements of our civilization and culture. We find them still as fresh as the first day and use them as either keys with which to open the long-locked doors of hearts, or the doors of castles on the way to conveying civilization to all parts of the world, or as torches of learning with which to illuminate the world. They are still so powerful and enchanting that while some of them introduce us into the world of Ibn Khaldun or Biruni or Zahrawi or Shafi'i, Abu Hanifa, Malik and Ibn Hanbal, some others bring us roses from the gardens of spiritual masters like Ibrahim ibn Adham, 'Abd al-Qadir al-Jilani, Shah Naqshband, Ahmad Badawi and Abu'l-Hasan al-Shadhili, and still others take us to the evergreen summits of Iqbal, Baqi, Fuduli, Sa'di, Nizami, Nawa'i and Rumi.

With its natural environment unpolluted and in good order and harmony, its lovely towns and villages re-planned and re-designed, and its population equipped with such human values and virtues as belief, love, knowledge, mutual loyalty and high morals, this world would be a place fit for joyful, sincere-hearted people to dwell in; a place where rivers of love and other sublime feelings flow; where works of the finest artistry appear side by side with those of the sciences into which religion has breathed a new life; a place where families dwell whose members are attached to one another with love, respect and compassion. Those destined to live in this world will find it a paradise-like place cleansed of all kinds of impurity and foulness, and purified of all kinds of misery and dissipation, where angelic souls fly around and all are for each and each is for all.

This world will convey meanings from the other world, and plains and mountains will radiate peace and contentment. Emotions will be much deeper and fed by eternity. In this world whose material is woven of belief, morals, knowledge and love, life will be more beneficial and nothing wasted.

We are now on the way to this world of love, peace and vitality. Our final destination is He, the One to Whom we have devoted our hearts. We are walking toward Him along the way He has established. With our trust placed in Him and relying on His favours, our struggle is to reach Him. He will produce the result, Who never breaks His word and always fulfils His promise. So why be hopeless? Why speak of thorns in the garden of roses?

We are servants chained at His doorway. He always makes us understand our servanthood. Our aim is to be able to perform the duty of thanksgiving for His making Himself known to us. We always seek refuge in His Court. He will surely admit those who, after long journeying, knock at the door of His Court. He will surely admit them to the final union.

ACTION AND THOUGHT

The line of struggle followed by the righteous people to whom God promised the future of the world may be summed up in two words: action and thought. In fact, the way to true existence is action and thought, and likewise the way to renewal, individual and collective. It may even be said that every being is the product of certain movements and disciplines and its continuance depends on the same.

Action should be the most indispensable element or feature of our lives. Even at the cost of many losses, we should take on necessary responsibilities and strive in action and thought continually to realize them. If we are unable to initiate action in the direction of our essential beliefs and concepts, we will inevitably fall under the influence of others and be carried away by the way of their actions and ideas, always reacting at the mercy of their initiatives.

Inertia and futile pessimism in the face of the events around us mean consenting to melt away like ice dropped in hot water. Such consent invites dissolution of the linked elements which make up our essence. It is passive submission to any formation alien or adverse to our essential identity. Those who desire the competence to remain truly themselves, should seek it wholeheartedly and with all their strength, and try to realize it in actual life. Existence and its continuance depend upon an inner tension and cohesion which (if authentic) will never decay; they require resistance, power, and the appropriate intellectual and spiritual equipment.

We should know how to be ourselves and then remain ourselves. That does not mean isolation from others. It means preservation of our essential identity among others, following our way among other ways. While self-identity is necessary, we should also find the ways to a universal integration. Isolation from the world will eventually result in annihilation. We must have nothing to do with ambitions such as realization of self-interests or attitudes that concentrate on selfish desires. Contentment for a man of true thought and action lies in the contentment of the whole being, in this world and the next. Therefore, he never conceives of restricting the sphere of activism to any particular time or space. Rather, he pursues goals that encompass all time and space. For this reason, he never considers any happiness restricted as to time or space or segment of creation as true happiness.

Action in this context then means embracing the whole of creation with full sincerity and resolve, aware of journeying to an eternal realm through the corridors in creation and equipped with a power from that infinite, eternal realm; it means expending all one's physical, intellectual and spiritual faculties in guiding the world to undertake the same journey.

As for thought, it is action in one's inner world. Any truly systematic thinking entails seeking answers to all questions arising from the existence of the universe as such. In other words, truly systematic thinking is the product of a conscious mind relating itself to the whole of creation and seeking the truth in everything through its language.

It is by means of thought that man's spirit becomes intimate and familiar with creation and continuously deepens through learning and experience. Escaping from the illusions and narrow confines of a mind only preoccupied with earning a livelihood, the spirit awakens to the absolute truths which never mislead. In other words, true thinking is equivalent to self purifying, to preparing in oneself room for metaphysical experiences. The last stage of thought is active thinking.

The basic dynamic of our life of action and thought is our spiritual life, which is based on our religious values. Just a rosebud turned towards light unfurls into an elaborate flower, so we, in the past, appeared as a great nation in the historical and international arena after we turned towards and embraced our religion. This overall self-attainment caused our potentials to develop and secured our existence for centuries. Again, just as our existence and self-attainment depend on attachment to our religion and its values, our integration with the whole of creation requires the same, as was the case in the past. Indeed, every act of a believer is worship, his every thought self-disicline, his every speech a supplication expressing his degree of knowledge of God, his every observation a research, and his relations with others a grounding in love and compassion. Spirituality of such degree and quality requires both intuition and logic, rationality and enlightenment and being open to Divine inspirations. In other words, it is difficult to realize unless experience is examined by reason, and reason accepts the authority of Divine guidance, and logic becomes identical with love, and love is transformed into love of God. Once spirituality of this degree is attained, sciences become a beam of light in the hand of inspiration which reaches everywhere, and the results of sense-experience and experimental knowledge become a prism reflecting the meaning of existence. Then, everything resounds with knowledge of God, love and songs of spiritual joy.

Those who are planning the happy world of the future should be aware that what kind of world they mean to build, what sort of jewels they should use in its construction, so that they will not have, later, to destroy with their own hands what their own hands built. Equipped with rational thought and religious values and historical dynamics, they should know how to apply the principles of the Qur'an and *Sunnah* and the judgements derived from them by conscientious scholars, to the world they intend to build. They should never be given over to carnal appetites and temporary aspirations. They should aim purely at gaining God's approval and strictly preserve the purity of their intention. They should never neglect to perform their religious duties: in prayers and supplications they should be aware that they are before One Who is nearer to them than themselves. They should do their prescribed prayers in the awareness that prayers are the believer's means of 'ascension'. They should fast for the pleasure of going to the 'union' with God. They should pay their alms-taxes in an attitude of returning to their rightful owner the goods entrusted to their keeping for a time. And they should the *Hajj* conscious of attending an international conference at which the problems of all the world's Muslims will be exposed and discussed in a place where the spirit can observe and experience the luminosity and awe of the higher realms of existence.

However, the realization of such noble aims depends on the existence of guides and leaders able to both diagnose our external and inner misery and to be themselve in constant relation with the higher worlds. There have always been and will always be such guides who have built all the true civilizations and they will again carry, by God's Will and Power, all movements of revival to victory. With their world of thought encompassing the material and spiritual, the physical and metaphysical, and philosophy and gnostic knowledge, those guides and leaders, who are perfectly aware of the requirements of time and circumstances, will develop new doctrines of law based on the Qur'an and *Sunnah*, integrate regional features with Islamic universals, inject a new spirit and give a new meaning to art, and unite what is modern with the traditional. Thus, all the institutions of life will be re-moulded and the coming generations provided with knowledge, skills and profound spirituality. Streets will become like school corridors, prisons (if any) will change into buildings of education and houses will be transformed into palaces of Paradise. Sciences will progress hand-in-hand with religion, and belief and reason combined will yield ever-fresh fruits of their cooperation. In short, the future will witness a new world built in the arms of hope, belief, love, knowledge, and resolve, a world more content and prosperous than the utopias dreamed of in the West.

No one should argue that we are far from such a world. Who knows? We may be on its threshold. The whole of mankind will see, in a near future, what other 'suns' will be born from the 'womb' of the night before the day breaks.

SELF-RENEWAL

Self-renewal is the first condition of survival. Those who cannot renew themselves when necessary face annihilation sooner or later, no matter how powerful they may be. Everything lives and continues to live through the effort of self-renewal. When renewal ceases – as it has ceased for a corpse – decomposition sets in.

The earth in springtime is a wonderful image and instance of universal renewal. Grass, trees and soil – in a thumbnail portion of which countless organisms are nurtured – all together come back to life. Take a walk amongst the living creatures – how they sally forth, putting on their uniforms of renewal and rejoicing in growth! How seemingly lifeless things come to life, like armies called out to parade, transforming the earth into a cheerful, multi-coloured paradise! Thus the spring shows innumerable signs of global renewal. Here a sentient, animate creature panting, heaving itself forward, in a mighty effort to achieve self-renewal. There, sprouting plant-forms pushing and struggling against whatever hardship surrounds them to emerge into the light in a cluster of shoots. And there, seeds scattered in thistle down, blown along with so many other kinds by winds obedient to the season, and pollen carried upon the legs of busy insects to fertilize the eager flowers, all alike actively seeking their renewal and continuance of life. And where the effort for self-renewal is not made, a decomposing and sinking back into the soil, there to be consumed without hope of renewed emergence.

Man too must, like every other creature, make the effort for self-renewal, individually and collectively. The more that communities and societies revive and rejuvenate themselves in mind and spirit, the better they are able to shoulder the world-wide responsibilities. That is accomplished by enlightening the sciences with the truth of religion, by applying technology with the wisdom of faith, and by carrying the message of revival to all people. Those communities who fail to renew themselves in this way will never be safe from destruction and the chains of captivity.

Self-renewal must not be confused, as it often is, with the indulgence of mere novelty and the latest fashions, which is mere cosmetic covering up of defects. True renewal is providing the community with immortality through the water of life from the fountain of Khadr – the saintly sage whose guidance is said to come to those who are worthy of it and grant them a kind of eternity.

True renewal is seeking and obtaining higher and purer levels of contemplation. It is preserving the purity of seed and root, of upholding the values refined and handed down over the centuries in association with the knowledge and ideas of modern times. It is sheer delusion to make outward forms of dress a measure of modernity or backwardness, and another delusion to suppose people will long be taken in by so shallow a criterion.

Self-renewal takes place in the metaphysical, not the physical, realm and is a revival of the spirit and of the spiritual life; the term 'renewal' is not seriously used for any other kind of renovation.

Renewal is true insofar as it engages in and uses modern scientific developments and technological facilities as means to increase our knowledge of the universe. However, we must constantly hold up to our hearts the mirror of self-examination so that our understanding is truly and meaningfully renewed.

An individual who has succeeded in renewing himself may

be considered an enduring support to the well-being of the community. A society which comprises many such individuals becomes an important element in the balance of the world. But certainly there cannot be a society-wide renewal without sufficient numbers of individuals who have truly renewed themselves. Such people have hearts radiant with faith and minds soaring into different realms in quest of 'bright days', people who each moment renew the quality of their consciousness of that which is holy and true. Further, it is necessary that individuals of this calibre be followed by successors willing and able to hold aloft their thoughts and ideals like a torch.

The Ummayyads were unable to save themselves from destruction at the hands of powerful rivals because, as a dynasty, they proved incapable of carrying on the revival of 'Umar ibn 'Abd al-'Aziz: they wallowed in corruption and passed away in humiliation. Almost the same is true of the Abbasids, and of the Ummayyads in Andalusia, and of the Ottoman Turks of the 18th century. These magnificent states decayed and disintegrated in a similar manner, at the same time receiving heavy blows from external enemies. They applied themselves to Latin and Greek philosophy in the hope of sparking a renewal of their spirit thereby. This proved no remedy at all, rather it accelerated their destruction. Worse, in the case of the Ottomans, it caused them to deviate from their essential line of development and engage in a mindless imitativeness of their enemies so that the Ottoman intelligentsia became something of a laughing-stock in Europe.

Neither the 'New Regime' which, under Selim III reorganized the imperial army on a french model, nor the massacre of the Janissaries, nor the Imperial Edict proclaimed in Gulhane Park in the time of Sultan 'Abd al-Majid by some callow and fanciful imitators of the West who sought to institute political reforms, were able to open the road to a revival for the Ottoman society. Indeed, the reverse is true, that such measures stifled that society and threw it into a death-like coma. We do not deny that there were some positive aspects to these movements but these were of so localized a nature as to have no bearing on the negative outcome. It can even be argued that the evident weaknesses of the Ottoman regime, disguised by these reforms, became thereby more insidious and therefore more dangerous. Such inappropriate remedies had no more long-term usefulness than sedating a patient suffering convulsions or applying a truss to a hernia.

Almost all the promises made by such dead, unintelligent souls who had lost their own way have proved a delusion which led, and continues to lead, the ordinary mass of people astray. I do not know whether we shall be able to teach true renewal to those who have been, over and over again, deceived and misled.

SACRED EMIGRATION

Emigration is an important phenomenon in human history. Besides its general relevance to the establishment of civilizations, it has special significance in connection with the 'holy ones', those chosen to carry light throughout the world.

First of all, every individual is a traveller and therefore, in some sense, an emigrant. His journeying starts in the world of spirits and continues through the stations of his mother's womb, childhood, youth, old age and his grave, and from there to a completely new world. Although he is among millions of people, each individual is born alone, lives his own life, endures his own death, and will be resurrected alone. Likewise, each of those men of high stature who throughout history have guided mankind, started his sacred mission from his single self, then disseminating light from the torch he carried and illumining the minds and hearts of others, inculcating hope and faith in his followers and transforming the lands once submerged in darkness into pools of light. And each one of these guides had to emigrate from one place to another for the sake of his cause.

Belief, emigration and holy struggle are the three pillars of a single, sacred truth. They are the three 'taps' of a fountain from which the water of life flows for the 'holy ones' to drink from so that they may convey their message without being wearied, and, when the opposition is too formidable to overcome, set out for a new land without regard for their home, property or family.

However sacred the cause, however useful and original the

thoughts or brilliant the message, those who hear it for the first time are naturally bound to question and oppose it. For this reason, the one who wants to arouse the people to new sentiments, new faith, new love and new ideas must either persist in his mission in his homeland in the face of all kinds of resistance, or set out for new minds and hearts to pour out his inspirations and offer his message to.

Every new idea or message has always been resisted where it has appeared, and those who have offered it have usually been welcomed in new places where their pasts were unknown. It is for this reason that the fate of the 'holy ones' is almost the same: they begin with belief and love, followed by struggle against the deviation and error of the masses, and then comes the turn of emigration for the sake of the well-being of mankind, even at the cost of sacrificing their own homes and families.

In every movement of revival, prior to emigration, two stages are of great importance. In the first stage, a man with a cause develops his character, overflows with belief and is inflamed with love, and surpassing his own self, grows into a passionate slave of truth. He struggles, in this stage, against the temptations of his carnal self to build his authentic, spiritual character. This is called 'the major or greater struggle' – *al-jihad al-akbar*. Then he rises, in the second stage, to radiate the lights of belief to the world around him. This stage is, in fact, the door to emigration.

Emigration should not, of course, be understood only in the material sense. Rather, a man experiences emigration throughout his life in the spiritual sense. Each inner intellectual or spiritual transformation, from indolence to action, from decay to self-renewal, from suffocation in the atmosphere of sinfulness to exaltation in the realm of spirit, may be regarded as an emigration. It is my conviction that only those who have been able to actualize these inner emigrations can find in themselves the strength and resolution to leave their homes and families for the sake of a sublime ideal. It is almost impossible for those who have not succeeded in 'emigrating' from the carnal self to the realm of spirit, from the pomp and luxury of the world to the riches of intellect and spirit, and from the pleasures of selfhood to an altruistic life, to emigrate for the good and welfare of humanity.

Emigration with its two dimensions, spiritual and material, was first represented by the great Prophets, Abraham, Lot, Moses and Jesus, upon them be peace, who shone like suns on the horizon of humanity, and in its most comprehensive meaning and function, was realized by the greatest of them, namely the Prophet Muhammad, who is the pride of mankind, upon him be peace and blessings. The door to emigration has since been open to all those who would walk in his footsteps.

Emigration in the way of truth and for its sake is so sanctified that the community of holy ones around the Last Prophet, who sacrificed their possessions and souls for the sake of the cause they believed in, and of the matchless representative of that cause, were praised by God as (and have since been called) 'the Emigrants'. We can see its importance in the fact that the beginning of the sacred era of this holy community was marked, not by the birth of the Prophet or by the first revelation or such victories as Badr or the conquest of Makka, but by the emigration to Madina.

Every individual who has emigrated for the sake of a sublime ideal will always deeply feel the pressure of the ideal which urged him to emigrate and design his life according to that ideal. Secondly, he will be freed from the criticism regarding some faults he might have made in childhood or youth. Whereas, in his own land, he is probably remembered and criticized for past faults, and has little influence upon people because, besides the factors mentioned, he is already familiar to them; in the land he has emigrated to, he will be known for his spiritual brilliance, unadulterated ideas, pure intentions and extraordinary sacrifices. For these and other reasons, it has almost always been emigrants who changed the flow of history and started new eras in the life of humanity.

Toynbee, the renowned British historian, mentions twenty-seven civilizations founded by nomadic or migrant peoples. This is because no one can overcome such dynamic people. They are not habituated to ease and comfort, are ready to sacrifice everything worldly, used to every kind of hardships, and always ready to march wherever their cause requires them to go.

The 'holy ones' around the Last Prophet, who were elevated from the darkness of ignorance and savagery to become the founders of the most brilliant civilization in human history and the first teachers of a universal religion, which is still the hope of mankind for a happy future, set the best example in this matter for those coming after them. Those who later walked in their footsteps found ease and serenity in fighting with difficulties, and found vigour and life in despising death and everything worldly, and eternity in constant renewal in thought, spirit and action. They migrated from land to land to convey knowledge, morality and civilization everywhere that they settled.

It is incumbent upon us to save the young generation from indulgence and attachment to the comfort of life, and in doing so to equip them with lofty ideals so that they know how to suffer with the pains and sorrows of mankind. It is only when this is accomplished to a significant degree that our old world will be able to witness an overall felicity.

OUR SYSTEM OF EDUCATION

Our minds naturally turn to the quality of schools and teachers when a new school year starts. But we should not be able to help thinking about it constantly since schooling is so vital a part of the making of human beings. A school may be considered as a laboratory in which an elixir is offered which can prevent or heal the ills of life, and teachers are the masters by whose skills and wisdom the elixir is prepared and administered.

The school is a place of learning, where everything related to this life and the next can be learnt. It can shed light on vital ideas and events and enable its students to understand their natural and human environment. It can also quickly open the way to unveiling the meaning of things and events, which leads man to wholeness of thought and contemplation. In essence the school is a kind of place of worship whose 'holy men' are teachers.

Good schools worthy of the name are pavilions of angels, which develop feelings of virtue in their pupils and lead them to achieve nobility of mind and spirit. As to the others, however soundly built they may appear, they are in fact ruins – they instil false ideas into their pupils,· turning out monsters. Such schools are nests of snakes, and we should be consumed with shame that they are called places of learning.

The real teacher is one who sows the pure seed and preserves it. It is his duty to be occupied with what is good and wholesome, and to lead and guide the child in his or her life and in the face of all events. As it is in the school that life, flowing outside in so many different directions, acquires a stable character and identity, so too it is in the school that a child is cast in his or her true mould and attains to the mysteries of personality. Just as a wide, full river gains force as it flows in a narrow channel, so too, the flowing of life in undirected ways is channelled into unity by means of the school. In like manner, a fruit is a manifestation of unity growing out of the fruit-tree's diversity.

School is thought to be relevant only in a particular phase of life. However, it is much more than that. It is essentially the 'theatre' in which all the scattered things of the universe are displayed together. It provides its pupils with the possibilities of continuous reading and speaks even when it is silent. Because of that, although it seems to occupy one phase of life, actually the school dominates all times and events. Every pupil re-enacts during the rest of life what he or she has learnt at school and derives continuous influence therefrom. What is learned or acquired at school may either be imagination and aspirations, or specific skills and realities. But what is of importance here is that everything acquired must, in some mysterious way, be the key to closed doors, and a guidance to the ways to virtue.

Information rightly acquired at school and fully internalized by the self, is a means by which the individual rises beyond the clouds of this gross world of matter and reaches to the borders of eternity. Information not fully internalized by the self is no more than a burden loaded upon the pupil's back. It is a burden of responsibility on its owner, and a devil which confuses the mind. That kind of information which has been memorized but not fully digested does not provide light to the mind and elevation to the spirit, but remains simply a nuisance to the self.

The best sort of knowledge to be acquired in the school must be such that it enables pupils to connect happenings in the outer world to their inner experience. The teacher must be a guide who can give insight into what is experienced. No doubt the best guide (and one that continually repeats its lessons) is life itself. Nevertheless, those who do not know how to take a lesson directly from life need some intermediaries. These intermediaries are the teachers – it is they who provide the link between life and the self, and interpret the manifestations of life's happenings.

The mass media can communicate information to human beings, but they can never teach real life. Teachers are irreplaceable in this respect. It is the teachers alone who find a way to the heart of the pupil and leave indelible imprints upon his or her mind. Teachers who reflect deeply and impart the truths will be able to provide good examples for their pupils and teach them the aims of the sciences. They will test the information they are going to pass on to their pupils through the refinement of their own minds, not by such Western methods as are today thought to provide facile answers to everything.

The students of the Prophet Jesus, upon him be peace, learnt from him how to risk their lives for the sake of their cause and were able to endure being thrown into the mouths of lions: they knew that their master had persisted with his teachings even in the face of death threats. Those who put their hopes on, and gave their hearts to, the Prophet Muhammad, the greatest exemplar of humanity, upon him be peace and blessings, realized that suffering for the sake of truth resulted in peace and salvation. His students observed their master wish peace and felicity for his enemies even when he had been severely injured by them.

A good lesson is what is taught at the school by the real teacher. This lesson not only provides the pupil with something, but it also elevates him or her into the presence of the unknown. The pupil thus acquires a penetrating vision into the reality of things and sees each event as a sign of the unseen worlds.

At such a school one is tired of neither learning nor teaching, because the pupils, through the increasing zeal of their teacher, sometimes rise to the stars. Sometimes their consciousness overflows the boundaries of ordinary life, brimming with wonder at what they have thought or felt or experienced.

The real teacher seizes the landmarks of events and happenings and tries to identify the truth in everything, expounding it by using every possibility.

Rousseau's teacher was conscience; Kant's was conscience together with reason... In the school of the Mawlana and Yunus, the teacher was the Prophet Muhammad, upon him be peace and blessings. The Qur'an is the recitation, its words are Divine lessons – they are not ordinary words but mysterious ones surpassing all others, and they manifest the highest unity in multiplicity.

The good school is the holy place where the light of the Qur'an will be focused, and the teacher is the magic master of this mysterious laboratory. The only true master is one who will save us from centuries-old pains, and, by the strength of his wisdom, remove the darkness covering our horizon.

THE NEW MAN

Within the movement of history we have been carried to the threshold of a new age open to the manifestations of Divine favour. Despite (or in parallel with) the advances in science and technology, the last two or three centuries have witnessed, across the world, a break with traditional values and, in the name of renewal, attachment to different values and speculative fantasies. However, it is our hope, strengthened by promising developments all over the world, that the next century will be the age of belief and moral values, an age that will witness a 'renaissance' and revival for the believers throughout the world.

Among wavering crowds, lacking in sound thinking and reasoning, a new kind of man will appear, who relies equally on reason and experience, and who gives as much importance to conscience and inspiration as he does to reason and experience. He is a man who unfailingly pursues the perfect in everything, and is able to establish the balance between this world and the next, and wed the heart to the intellect.

The coming to be of a man as new as this will not be easy. Every birth is painful, but this blessed birth will certainly take place and the world will have a new, brilliant generation. Just as rain does pour out of long gathering clouds, and water does well up from the depths of earth, so too will the 'flowers' of this new generation sooner or later appear among us.

The new man is a person of integrity who, free from external influences, can manage independently of others. No worldly force can hold him in captivity, no fashionable isms cause him to deviate from his path. Truly independent of any worldly power, he thinks freely and acts freely, and his freedom is in proportion to his servanthood to God. Rather than imitating others in passing fancies, he relies on his original dynamics, rooted in the depths of history, and tries to equip his faculties of judgement with values authentically his own.

He is one who thinks, investigates, and believes, and overflows with spiritual pleasures. While able to make the fullest use of modern facilities, he does not neglect his traditional and spiritual values in building his own world.

If changes and reforms are linked to and dependent on unchanging universal values, they may be eagerly welcomed. Otherwise, there will be a chaos of speculative fantasies appealing only on account of novelty and modernity. Standing on the firm ground of those unchanging values, the new man always looks to the future to illuminate the darkness enveloping the world. He is truth-loving and trustworthy to the utmost degree and, in order to support the truth everywhere, he will be ready, whenever necessary, to leave his family and home. Having no attachment to worldly things, comforts and luxuries, he will use whatever he was endowed with by God for the benefit of humankind and sow the world with the seeds of a happy future. Then, seeking help from God and in never-ending hope of success from Him, he will do his best to protect those seeds from harm, with the same care that a hen protects the eggs it is incubating. He will dedicate his whole life to this way of truth.

In order to stay in touch and communicate with the minds, hearts and feelings of people, the new man will make use of mass media, and try to establish in the world a new power balance on the foundations of justice, love, respect and equality between human beings. He will put might under the command of right and never discriminate on grounds of colour or race.

The new man will unite in his character profound spirituality, wide knowledge, sound thinking, a scientific temperament, and wise activism. Never content with what he already knows, he will continuously increase in knowledge – knowledge of the self, knowledge of nature, and knowledge of God.

Equipped with good morals and virtues which make a man truly human, the new man is an altruist, who embraces all humanity with his love and is ever ready to sacrifice himself for the good of others. As he shapes himself in the mould of universal virtues, he strives at the same time to illuminate the way of others. He always defends and supports what is good, and commends it to others, while he tries to challenge, combat and eradicate all evils.

The new man believes that the One who has given him existence in this world, has done this so that he should know Him and worship Him. Without discriminating between the book of the universe (which is the place of the manifestation of Divine Names and therefore full of signs to Him and a 'stairway' leading to Him) and the Divine Scripture (which is the translation of the book of the universe), the new man sees religion and science as two kinds of manifestation of the same truth.

The new man is never reactionary. He does not go after events, rather being the motor of history, he initiates and shapes events, and with due perception of his age and the conditions surrounding him and in devotion to his essential values and utmost reliance on God, he is in a state of continuous self-renewal.

The new man is a conqueror and discoverer: conqueror of himself, conqueror of thoughts and conqueror of hearts, and discoverer of what is all unknown in the universe. He regards that time as wasted when he is not taking a new step into the depths of the self and the universe. As he removes, through his faith and knowledge, the veils that cover the face of reality, he feels more eager to advance further with the messages and answers he receives from the heavens, the earth and seas, he continues on his journey which goes on until he returns unto his Creator.

THE AWAITED GENERATION

We have long been awaiting a generation, with hearts as pure and kind as angels, with will-power strong enough to overcome the most formidable obstacles, and minds keen enough to solve all the problems of the age. Had it not been for the persistence of our hope for the coming of such a blessed generation, we would long ago have been a thing of the past.

We live in the darkest of nights until they appear on our horizon with radiant faces promising the breaking of dawn. Once they have appeared on our horizon, this land of the wretched and the miserable, resembling a gloomy graveyard, will begin to be cheered by flowers of every kind. If our hopes are not blighted by a poisonous wind, this land, changing into a flower-garden through the reviving water that that generation brings, will be a place of happiness and 'spiritual recreation' for all the world's people, a place of peace, harmony and serenity. The world of the future will be so enlightened by their light that the moon and the sun will be dim in comparison. In their enlightened ethos, the universe will be studied as a meaningful book and the music of brotherhood will be played everywhere. Art and literature will be refined of coarseness and vulgarities of all kinds and find noble-minded practitioners.

This world will indeed be built anew when they sound the note of revival, and those who fell into a kind of winter sleep will wake up. The music of despair composed by Satan and played by some indolent persons will stop; people will be exhilarated with melodies of hope and activity which they compose and play.

The awaited generation are successors to the mission of the master of the Prophets, and therefore have inherited the loyalty and faithfulness of Adam, the resolve and steadfastness of Noah, the devotion and gentleness of Abraham, the valour and dynamism of Moses, the forbearance and compassion of Jesus. When found together in a group, these qualities are such a great source of power that those who have them will inevitably seize the 'reins' of the world, provided they remain loyal to the covenant God has made with them.

The world is to be saved by that 'golden' generation who represent the Divine Mercy, from all the disasters, intellectual, spiritual, social and political, with which it has long been afflicted. The world will come back, through their efforts, to its 'primordial' pattern, on which God created it, and be purified of all kinds of deviation and ignorance, so that people may rise to 'the highest of the high' on the ladder of belief, knowledge and love, supported against the heavens by the Divine Message.

Humankind have never been so wretched as they are today. They have lost all their values: the 'table of art and literature' is 'vandalized' by drunks; thought is capital wasted in the hands of people suffering from intellectual poverty; science is a plaything of materialism; and the products of science are tools used in the name of unbelief. Amid such disorder and bewilderment, the people neither know their destination in the world nor the direction to follow to reach that destination.

In order to awaken the people and guide them to truth, the awaited generation, those young people who implant hope in our hearts, enlighten our minds and quicken our souls, will suffer with the sufferings of humankind and 'water' all the 'barren lands' with the tears they shed over centuries-old miseries. They will visit every corner of the world, leaving no-one not called upon, and pour out their reviving inspirations into the souls of the dumbstruck people. Having so long awaited those holy ones, sound-minded, saintly and trustworthy, who have dedicated themselves to humankind, the people will at last feel able to take the road to the depths of the heavens and reach eternity.

O long-awaited generation! Rise, for the love of the Creator, to your sacred task, and replace the choking darkness around us with the light of your love, hope and nobility! Rise and force back the 'monsters' of the age to their dens! Even if the world unites against you in the form of a terrible bomb; even if they upset your plans and systems; even if they make concerted attacks upon you from all sides, you will never quake; rather, with undiminished hope, you will continue to pave the way for the happy future. You will, like the Prophet Solomon, ride the winds and bring rain to the barren lands in order to change them into flower gardens. You will put an end to injustice all over the world and run to the aid of the oppressed; be so forbearing towards people that there will be no soul you have not embraced, no vengeance or rancour you have not removed.

O you who have been awaited for centuries! Look! Darkness is disappearing from your horizon and different melodies are being heard from beyond it. Those melodies, reaching us in the early hours of the 'morning' will spread throughout the world in the coming days. If you suspect that this is 'false dawn' – though it is not – do not be grieved as even a false dawn promises the 'true dawn'.

Rejoice and sing the praises of the happy future! Let your souls overflow with the glad tidings of that future, and let your eyes be filled with tears of happiness! I hope that your centuries-old longings are about to come to an end, and you are at the mysterious door opening to a spiritual world. Now you should bow before your Lord humbly, acknowledging your innate powerlessness, then set out for eternity with love, zeal and energy, so that you may deserve His help and exhilarating company during your journey, and watch the beauties displayed by Him.

When you reach, in such spirituality, the door of the Eternal World, the angels will welcome you, saying, *Peace be upon you! Well have you done! Enter you here, to dwell therein forever!* You will respond to this welcome with gratitude and say: *Praise be to God, Who has truly fulfilled His promise to us, and given us the earth to inherit, and that we may dwell in Paradise wherever we desire.*

THE SPIRIT OF STRUGGLE

Belief, with the will-power to struggle, is the first and foremost condition for success in life. Those who have prospered in heart with belief and developed in mind to produce pure and lofty thought, find in each second of their life a different type of happiness and can sense something like the life in gardens of Paradise. As for the souls who are devoid of such belief and power of struggle, they are subject to despair and discouragement in the face of even the least difficulties.

Life requires striving and struggle if it is to be successful. This, in turn, requires equipping oneself with enough will-power and hope, and making sufficient preparations. Those who start without the proper equipment and due preparations will inevitably either be entangled in the confusing labyrinths of life or not be able to free themselves from imitating others blindly. They are, in either case, in a despised, miserable state and, even though they console themselves at times with types of false happiness, can never be saved from humiliation and wretchedness.

People such as those will not be freed from misery and contempt by possessing castles and palaces, and heaps of gold or money; for wealth 'rules' those unaware of their true being and drives them to indulgences, even if it may be a useful means for souls of integrity.

People mostly pursue easy aims and pleasures and therefore deprive themselves of great and true successes and lasting ben-

efits obtained through efforts and sincerity and through enduring hardships and troubles.

Those whose will-power is paralysed and who are devoid
of lofty ideals and altruism, hate striving and always seek an
easy life. They would like to spend their time untroubled and
expect their desires to be satisfied by magic. As they are faint-
hearted and self-seeking, they are always carried along by the
course of events and therefore are never constant in their views,
feelings and choices. In such fickleness they can neither maintain their identity, nor find true peace and happiness in life.
Like a quantity of still water in a small enclosed area, they will
ultimately 'dry up', giving no sign of life.

However, any effort exerted to preserve one's essential identity is, in fact, a source of true pleasure, as well as being a sacred attempt to securing happiness in the future. In order to experience this pleasure, one should remain faithful to one's
spiritual roots and cultivate belief and virtues. Those who cannot base their thoughts on these fundamental principles will
never be able to feel that lofty pleasure.

One of the problems of the greatest urgency facing us today
is to revive the young generations who, being devoid of any
ideal, are carried away by every novel ideology, by implanting
in them belief, patience, resolution, love of work, respect for the
past and zeal to build a happy future. Every effort exerted in
this cause will receive great acclaim as a sacred attempt to build
up both 'today' and 'tomorrow', and remain as a 'beautiful
memory' among future generations.

As it is vain to expect a harvest without first sowing the
land, so it is impossible to obtain our objectives without the sacrifices needed to raise the young generations to rank of true humanity. We should know how to 'give' before 'receiving', so
that we will be able to receive doubled and re-doubled in the
season of harvest.

A gardener who takes proper care of his garden tends the whole of it, not leaving out even a square inch, and plants it with fruit trees and different varieties of vegetables and flowers. Then, he waters them and feeds them, and prunes them. All these together are what an ideal gardening requires.

Now, I ask myself whether we can take the same care of the young generations in order to protect them from all kinds of deviation. Can we shelter them from continuous 'attacks' from within and without? In the efforts we exert in this cause, can we exhibit a sufficient degree of conviction, resolution and will-power? Indeed, it is not impossible for us, if we are willing to, to build up our life anew in different, greater dimensions and gain a new view of things and events, strengthening our will-power and gaining greater constancy. However, there is a single way or condition to accomplish this: we should direct our will-power in a way deserving of the aid and blessings of the Truth.

If we can perceive the world we live in and set up the balance-wheels of our hope and will-power according to the standards established by the Infinite One, we will be able to breast the waves of life and overcome all kinds of difficulties and obstacles. Nothing will be able to hinder us from reaching our goal, and, without being influenced by the passage of seasons and changing of circumstances, we will remain ever-fresh and ever-shining in our climate of belief, hope and resolution.

RELIGIOUS FESTIVALS

Almost every nation has religious festivals to commemorate important events in their history or to celebrate special occasions.

There are two religious festivals in Islam, *'Id al-Fitr*, the festival of the breaking of the fast at the end of the month of Ramadan, during which Muslims fast from dawn until sunset. *'Id al-Adha*, the festival of sacrifice, comes on the tenth of *Dhu'l-Hijjah*, the last month of the Islamic year in which the pilgrimage is performed. Both festivals enjoy a very special place in the life of Muslims and leave indelible impressions on the culture of Muslim peoples.

Religious festivals for Muslims are times of deepened Islamic thoughts and feelings when memories of a long and honourable past are revived, recalled and 'lived' afresh with all their joys and sorrows.

Religious festivals are, for Muslims, occasions of paradoxical feelings – pangs of separation and hopes of re-union, regrets and expectations, and joys and sorrows. While, on the one hand, they feel sadness over losses in either individual or national spheres, on the other, they feel, paradoxically, the exhilarating pleasure of an expected revival, like the revival of nature in spring after a severe winter.

Muslims enjoy the pleasure of re-union and of a universal brotherhood on festival days. They smile at each other lovingly, greet each other respectfully, and pay visits to each other. Members of divided families whom the modern, industrialized life has forced to live apart from each other in different towns, come together and enjoy the delight of eating, together once more, and living, once again, a few days together.

Religious festivals are, for Muslims, occasions for spiritual revival through seeking God's forgiveness and through His praise and glorification. They are enraptured by special supplications, odes and eulogies for the Prophet, upon him be peace and blessings. Especially in traditional circles where the traces of the past are still alive, people experience the meaning of the festival in a more vivid, colourful fashion, on cushions or sofas, or around stoves or fire-places in their humble houses or cottages, or under the trees among the flowers in their gardens, or in the spacious halls of their homes. They feel the meaning of the festival in each morsel they eat, in each sip they drink and in each word they speak about their traditional and religious values.

Religious festivals are of a much greater significance for children. They feel a different joy and pleasure in the warm, embracing climate of the festivals, which they have been preparing to welcome a few days before, and, like nightingales singing on branches of trees, they cause us to experience the festivals more deeply through their play, their songs, smiles and cheerfulness.

Religious festivals provide the most practical means for improving human relationships. People experience a deep inward pleasure. They meet and exchange good wishes in a blessed atmosphere of spiritual harmony. It is especially when the festival permeates hearts with prayer and supplications performed consciously that souls are elevated to the realm of eternity. They then feel the urge to get rid of the clutches of worldly attachments and live in the depths of their spiritual being. In the atmosphere overflowing with love and mercy, a new hope is injected with life.

Believing souls welcome the religious festivals with wonder and expectations of otherwordly pleasures. It is, indeed, difficult to understand fully what believing souls feel during the religious festivals in the depths of their hearts. To perceive the feelings that the festivals arouse in pure souls who lead their life in ecstasies of otherworldly pleasures, it is necessary to experience such pleasures in the same degree.

Having reached the day of the festival after fulfilling their prescribed duty and responsibility, these souls display such a dignity and serenity, such a grace and spiritual perfection that those who see them think that they have all received a perfect religious and spiritual education. Some of them are so sincere and so devoted to God that each seems to represent the outcome of a long glorious history and to be the embodiment of centuries-old universal values. One may experience through their conduct and manners that taste of the fruits of Paradise, the peaceful atmosphere on the slopes of *firdaws* – the highest abode in Paradise – and the delight of being near to God.

VICTORY OF THE SPIRIT

Human life in this world is a composite of two distinct powers, the spirit and the flesh. Although it is sometimes the case that these two powers act in harmony, conflict between them is more usual, and conflict of a kind in which the victory of one results in the defeat of the other. In an individual in whom bodily lusts are vigorously indulged, the spirit grows more powerless as it becomes more obedient to those lusts; while in another individual, one who has given the spirit dominance over the flesh, in whom the heart (the seat of spiritual intellect) has power over reason, and the bodily lusts are vigorously opposed, it attains to eternity.

Every part of a spiritually bankrupt country can be likened to a graveyard, no matter how many hundreds of triumphal arches and statues adorn its thoroughfares. The mass of people living in such a country are in reality blind and unfortunate, and a world not built on the breath of the spirit is nothing but the plaything of human violence. A culture which has not developed an ethos that encourages virtue is like an evil sorceress who has ambushed humanity. However, it may never be possible to persuade coarse, insensitive people of this, people who pay no attention to anything except their own pleasures, who have become incapable of considering their lives as connected with the well-being and happiness of others. If only such people had had some perception of the mystery of their own deaths, they might yet have attained to the eternal life of the spirit.

Only those who have filled their hearts with the most sublime ideals and love of humanity will lead a spiritual life so as to attain to eternity in their very selves. They are the fortunate ones who have transcended their carnal desires, who have grown spiritually alert, and led those who heed them to victory over the commands of self.

Only he who overcomes his self can rightly be called powerful and victorious. The miserable individuals who have not been able to release themselves from captivity to the self are liable to defeat even if they had conquered the entire world. Moreover, we would not give to their conquest of the world the name of 'victory', since their permanent presence in the lands they invaded is an impossibility

Napoleon, in the madness of esteeming himself sole ruler of the world, slapped knowledge and virtue in the person of the philosopher, Molmey. I wonder whether he was able to grasp that this failure in spirit was more bitter and humiliating than his defeat at Waterloo. Mustafa Pasha of Merzifon had been inwardly defeated before his army was put to flight at Vienna. This first defeat in Ottoman history showed itself in the spirit of the commander-in-chief, then spread far and wide among his forces and not only caused him to lose his head, but allowed the greatest army of conquest the world had yet known to experience flight. Yildirim Khan, Bayazed I, was not defeated in Jubuk, but on the day when he belittled his opponent and hailed himself sole ruler of the world. And there have been many others like these...

But we have positive examples also. Tariq was victorious, not when he defeated the Spaniards' army of ninety thousand men with a handful of self-sacrificing valiants, but when he stood before the wealth and treasures of the king and said: 'Be careful, Tariq. You were a slave yesterday. Today you are a victorious commander. And tomorrow you will he under the earth.' Selim I regarded the world as too small for two rulers. He was truly victorious, not when he crowned some kings and dethroned others, but when he entered the capital in silence while its people were asleep so as to avoid their enthusiastic welcome and applause for his victories. He was also victorious when he ordered that the robe which had been soiled by the mud from the horse of his teacher be draped over his coffin because of its holiness. Cato, the Roman commander, was victorious and made a place for himself in the remembrance of his people, not when he defeated the Carthaginians, but when he handed his horse and command over to the Roman Emperor, saying: 'I fought to serve my nation. Now my duty is fulfilled, I am going back to my village'. And all the while his army was entering Carthage, the capital city of Rome's enemy and rival, in triumph.

To sacrifice one's enjoyment of worldly pleasures has the same significance for human progress as the roots of a tree have for its growth. Just as a tree grows sound and strong in direct relation to the soundness and strength of its roots, so too a human being grows to perfection while striving to free himself from selfishness, and, to live instead only for others.

These are the words of a sacred hymn signifying the victory of the spirit: 'I have known nothing of worldly pleasures in my life of over eighty years. All my life has passed on battlefields, in prisons and in various places of suffering. There is no torment which I have not experienced and no oppression which I have not suffered. I neither care for Paradise, nor fear Hell. If I thereby witness that the faith of my people has been secured, I will not object to burning in the flames of Hell, for my heart will change into a rose and a rose garden even as my body is being burnt.'

The crowned heads of the future will be those fortunate ones who have attained to felicity through victories of the spirit.